D0372174

You Shall Be My Witnesses

Lessons Beyond Dachau

Archbishop Kazimierz Majdański

Introduction by Carl A. Anderson
Translation by Maria Klepacka-Środoń

SQUAREONE
PUBLISHERS

The Biblical passages contained in this book have been translated from the Polish edition of the Bible, and may vary from the English version. While the words may be somewhat different, the concepts and meanings still hold true.

Cover Designer: Jeannie Tudor
Editor: Anna Comstock
Typesetter: Gary A. Rosenberg

Square One Publishers
Garden City Park, NY 11040
(516)535-2010
www.squareonepublishers.com

Publisher's Cataloging-in-Publication Data
Majdanski, Kazimierz.
  [Bedziecie moimi swiadkami. English]
  You shall be my witnesses / Kazimierz Majdanski ; translated from Polish by Maria Klepacka-Srodon.
       p. cm.
  ISBN 978-0-7570-0223-6
  1. Majdanski, Kazimierz. 2. Dachau (Concentration camp) 3. World War, 1939-1945—Personal narratives, Polish. 4. World War, 1939-1945—Religious aspects—Catholic Church. 5. Catholic Church—Poland—Clergy—Biography. 6. Prisoners of war—Poland—Biography. 7. Prisoners of war—Germany—Biography. I. Title.
  D805.5.D33M3513 2008
  940.53'18092—dc22
  [B]
                                2008038975

Printed in the United States of America

10   9   8   7   6   5   4   3   2   1

Contents

To Those Whose Witness I Was

Translator's Notes

I was asked by the author, Archbishop Majdański, to take up the task of translating *You Shall Be My Witnesses* into English during a personal interview he granted to me. The interview took place in the wake of much anti-Polish historical propaganda, which he had heard was being spread in the English-speaking world. At the time I was just a student at Cambridge University, and was about to move to Poland. Since then, I have completed many translation projects, but none have engraved themselves so strongly on my heart. I believe it was an enormous privilege and challenge that this was the first book I ever took up as an interpreter.

You Shall Be My Witnesses is more than just a personal testimony to the inhuman suffering borne by so many Polish priests who were persecuted especially for their faith at the hands of the inhuman Nazi regime. It is more than a personal account of being on the receiving end of pseudo-medical experiments carried out on prisoners by scientists who would then go on to make great careers—few of whom would ever be brought to justice. This book is more, because its testimony explicitly extends to the present reality of our own lives, and the threats that humanity continues to face in our own day.

The Archbishop saw families as the primary communities of life and love, and now as the primary arena of struggles for the Civilization of Love against the culture of death. He felt that now, instead of coming from public war machines, practices underpinned by disregard for human dignity are taking hold in many average homes, which are no longer welcoming or respectful of each other, or of the life of the children they conceive. The Archbishop knew the consequences of new laws drafted to accommodate degrading anti-human practices all too well, since he had been a victim of such "laws" and "orders" himself. He also knew what it meant when doctors departed from their vocation of serving the life and health of their patients in order to collaborate in anti-human practices, including abortion, sterilization, contraception, and artificial reproduction. These laws and practices desensitize the consciences of whole societies.

The Archbishop knew that even though the battlefield had changed, the struggle still existed, and he responded accordingly with exceptional foresight, strength, and perseverance. Not only did he found the first ever academic institute devoted to studies on the family, as well as an institute of lay consecrated life, the Holy Family Institute, but his last published essay—signed just three weeks before he died—was an ardent appeal to married couples to embrace the precepts set out in the papal encyclical *Humanae Vitae*, and to live the virtues of marital chastity and openness to life.

The Polish priests who survived Dachau and were liberated by a small contingent of American reconnaissance troops on April 29, 1945, all attributed their rescue to the aid of St. Joseph. Just before their liberation, they had pledged to St. Joseph that if they survived, they would become his instruments as guardians of families, just as he was once the guardian of the Holy Family. Furthermore, the extraordinary courage exhibited by the American troops that liberated the camps seems to support the belief that St. Joseph may have worked in a special way through them, as well. As Scriptures tell us, St. Joseph had to go beyond the law and overcome human fear to take up his task of protector and rescuer of the Holy Family. So too did the American troop commander. When he came across a train load of dead prisoners, he knew there must be a concentration camp nearby. Instead of retreating to seek further orders at that point, he followed the train tracks in the hope of rescuing any survivors. It appears that it was only thanks to his success in doing so that the remaining prisoners survived, because that day had been marked out by the Nazi regime for the ultimate eradication of all signs of the camp's existence—which of course would also have implied their extermination.

This exceptional act on the part of the liberators was later made evident when the troop commander was court-marshalled for his single-handed decision to go beyond his orders. Some of the prisoners he rescued heard of this, and traveled to give testimonies in his defense. Thankfully, he was acquitted in recognition of the courage, strength of heart, and faith he had shown in that defining moment. According to the Archbishop, the troop commander himself insisted that the prisoners first and foremost had God, not him, to thank for their liberation. *You Shall Be My Witnesses*, therefore, is a testimony of gratitude both to God and to the men He worked through. For American readers, it may be heartening to remember that this is a testimony that never would have been written and shared with us, but for the courage of a small group of American troops who followed their hearts to liberate the surviving Dachau inmates, as St. Joseph would surely have had them do.

Ultimately, *You Shall Be My Witnesses* is an edifying testimony of the victory of good over evil, a touching expression of thankfulness for survival and for life, and a testimony to first-hand experiences of heroic generosity, courage, and faithfulness to the priestly vocation, trust in God's mercy, and devotion to the Holy Mass. I agreed to take up the task of translating *You Shall Be My Witnesses* not only for the sake of historical truth, but also in the hope that this book would make the author and his story more accessible to the English-speaking world. My hope is that this book will help us to share Archbishop Majdański's perspective of our own contemporary struggles against what Pope John Paul II termed the Civilization of Death, and to respond accordingly by building the Civilization of Love.

Maria Klepacka–Srodoń
Executive Coordinator for Central
Europe of MaterCare International

Introduction

The scale of horror that took place in the Nazi death camps is literally overwhelming. The Nazis denied their prisoners' humanity in many ways, and ruthlessly executed millions of men, women, and children. Because we so often focus on the startling numbers of people that were murdered in these death camps, we are in danger of thinking of these victims as a faceless mass. But each victim was a human being, and while some are known to many of us—Anne Frank, Sopie Scholl, Elie Weisel, and Maximilian Kolbe, to name a few—the vast majority have been forgotten.

Forgotten too, in most of the world, is the Nazis' attempted obliteration of the cultures of occupied countries, and their paranoid reaction to any organized group perceived as constituting an ideological threat. In Poland, one of the groups the Nazis feared most was the Catholic Church. Because the Church was embedded in Polish society, with clergy well educated and respected by the people, the Nazis could not tolerate this institution in a country that they planned to radically redesign. Their goal, therefore, was to destroy it.

In his extraordinary memoir *You Shall Be My Witnesses*, Archbishop Kazimierz Majdański gives a voice and a face—his own—to the sufferings of the Polish people and the Polish clergy. Few things could be more terrifying than being a prisoner in the infamous

Dachau concentration camp. And in that camp of horrors, little could have raised the level of terror more than assignment to the medical experimentation section, where people—already given numbers and denied names—were further dehumanized and given less regard than animals. Yet as a young seminarian, Kazimierz Majdański experienced all of this—and survived. This book gives witness to his suffering.

The Archbishop's story chronicles what is—outside of Poland—an almost universally unknown element of the Nazi occupation of that country: the attempted destruction of Polish culture on a wholesale basis, and the systematic attack on the Polish clergy, who were seen as a threat to the Nazis' absolute totalitarian control. Through it all, Archbishop Majdański, as well as the priests and seminarians around him, never lost sight of the Christian's call to build a Civilization of Love. He never forgot his own humanity or that of those around him.

This memoir also chronicles Archbishop Majdański's close association with Karol Wojtyla, later Pope John Paul II, who also lived through this difficult period of Polish history. Through the Archbishop's words, we come to understand how Karol Wojtyla's own experience in the 1940s may have made him extraordinarily mindful of the dignity and value of each human person. From the depths of Nazi dehumanization, rose one of the greatest defenders of the dignity of every man, woman, and child.

One lesson stands out more than any other in Majdański's story: his forgiveness of the men who cruelly incarcerated him, callously experimented on him, and hated him for no reason other than his birth and faith. His ability to forgive—even more than his ability to physically survive—may well be the most remarkable aspect of this very unique story.

I will always remember my meetings with Archbishop Majdański, not only because he spoke of his own experiences and those of so many of his colleagues, but also because of the joyful and determined way in which he worked to better the lives of all those around him. Until his death, he remained a shining example of the vocation of the Christian—a vocation that at its heart testifies to the admonition of Saint Paul: "Do not be overcome by evil, but overcome evil with good." *(Rom. 12:21).*

That element of forgiveness in the face of such incredible circumstances demonstrates the best of Christianity in action. As Archbishop Majdański 's witnesses, we should all be motivated to follow his example of charity and forgiveness, so that the words "never again" will have a truly lasting meaning.

Carl A. Anderson
Supreme Knight
Knights of Columbus
New Haven, Connecticut

Witness

The task I have undertaken is an arduous one: to bear witness to those who witnessed, and to weigh in the balance the lived experience engraved on one's very soul.

I have long been obligated to bear witness. I was especially challenged to do this, however, at the beatification of Bishop Michael Kozal.[1] It was then, on August 14, 1986, that the Holy Father, Pope John Paul II, spoke to a group of Polish pilgrims at Castel Gandolfo:

> Today, on the eve of the Feast of the Assumption, we remember the blessed martyrdom of our countryman, Saint Maximilian Maria Kolbe.[2] . . . We offer to Our Blessed Lady not only our liturgical memories of Saint Maximilian, for it was this very day, on the eve of the Assumption, that she wished to call him to herself, to welcome this man who called himself a crusader of the Immaculate. For this reason, too, brothers and sisters, your presence, as my countrymen, is particularly dear to me. You come from different regions of Poland, my dear brothers in the priesthood. Especially dear to me is the presence of Your

Grace, Bishop Kazimierz Majdański, as you were a witness to similar experiences. . . . and you continue to be a witness for all of us, for the Church in Poland, and for the world.

Thus, in this book I decided to record my testimony in a manner more comprehensive than the fragmentary renderings I have given in the past. The task is a critical one, for it concerns witnesses whom Christ Our Lord Himself wishes to claim: "You shall be my witnesses . . . to the ends of the earth." *(Acts 1:8)*. At the same time, it concerns witnesses whose lives bore the following special mark of distinction: "They will hand you over to be tortured and put to death." *(Mt. 24:9)*.

My testimony recalls witnesses whom I knew from the beginning of the Second World War, through to its end—witnesses with whom I spent that whole time, both in prisons and in camps. The testimony centers mainly on Polish priests and seminarians, and especially on Bishop Michael Kozal, a fellow member of the episcopacy. Enriching this ministry with the fullness of the priesthood, he remained worthy of it even amid unspeakable suffering.

In advance, I must ask my lay camp-colleagues to forgive me in that, contrary to my wishes, I can only write of them from the perspective from that I saw them. This was the perspective of isolation, which was rigorously enforced by the prison guards, as well as the isolation that came from common suffering, which often left no breathing space in which to become closer to one another.

Insofar as it is possible, however, the testimony I intend to give will give witness to these lay people too. My narrative will unfold in the same spirit in which a group of Polish priests and bishops, which I had the honor to head, erected a commemorative plaque in Dachau in 1972. The plaque bears an inscription that outlines the concentration camp torment suffered by all of us Polish inmates—representatives of a nation condemned to extermination.[3]

The inscription reads in Polish, English, French, and German, as follows:

> Here in Dachau every third victim tormented to death was a Pole, and one in every two Polish priests imprisoned here laid down his life. Their sacred memory is venerated by their fellow prisoners, members of the Polish clergy.

We were joined by a group of Polish Protestant clergy in the concentration camp. They fully shared our prison lot with us, and this brought us mutually closer to each other.

I first began to commit this testimony to paper on November 11, 1986, exactly forty-four years from the moment when, as prisoner number 22 829, I was forced to undergo pseudo-medical research experiments. Much time has passed since that day. A further three years have passed from the time of my arrest on November 7, 1939 in Wloclawek, where I was later to become auxiliary bishop. Will my memory fail me? I must assure everyone who reads this testimony that my goal is to include in it all that I remember faithfully, bearing in mind my subjection to human error. On the other hand, the reflections prompted by these recollections have undoubtedly been tempered and tested by the distance of time. This should not, however, lessen their value.

Testimonies about the prison camp experiences of Polish clergymen have already been undertaken—notably by my seminary tutor, Bishop Francis Korszynski (1893–1962), in a book entitled *Bright Rays in Dachau*. This book is a reflection of his own unclouded soul; his recollections, therefore, constitute a contribution that merits much respect and gratitude. Its value is underlined by Cardinal Giovanni-Battista Montini's foreword to its Italian edition, and is also borne out by its exceptional popularity in Poland, where its second edition was rapidly exhausted.

My story begins with Wloclawek. This should not be surprising since the Wloclawek community, among Polish dioceses, takes a position of precedence in the Church's harvest of martyrdoms during the last war. Two great priests associated with this diocese must be singled out at the start. One of these was a participant in this holy sacrifice: Blessed Michael Kozal, bishop and martyr; the second was ordained a priest for that diocese, and became the ripe fruit of its history of martyrdom: Cardinal Stefan Wyszynski.[4] Many are praying for his beatification—for the elevation of this great Primate of the Millennium to the honors of the altar, I pray that this may soon come to be!

It remains, however, after so many years have passed, that there may be facts never committed to paper—facts that are now irretrievably lost to human memory. Even surnames have been forgotten, though thankfully they are secured in foreign and national registers. Registers are speechless, though; they have no voice but ours.

Ultimately, human words will always prove insufficient when intended to fulfill Christ's words: "You shall be my witnesses."

Since it is necessary to put pen to paper, though, let us begin, trusting in the help of Mary, Queen of Martyrs.

2

A Diabolical Ideology

What images will people's memories harbor when they reflect on the twentieth century? What will their image of twentieth-century Europe be? Europe had always played a leading role in the world, and despite the many changes this century brought forth, this continent has not lost its responsibility to the great legacy of history.

The center of the changes and aspirations of our times is marked by the human person, and progress, an attribute of man, has been invoked with extraordinary ambition.

Does the phrase "human person" denote an absolute? Many people in the twentieth century had come to think it did. Indeed, that is what one man, who came to believe he was a superhuman and a leader of *supermenschen* ("super men"), thought of himself. He was described as "mad," but nevertheless, this madman enslaved great masses of people and received homage's heretofore reserved for God. From time to time, the "non-humans" held in concentration camps would be given the "honor" of waiting interminably on the parade ground to hear him speak. It was not the hysteria of the speaker that was most terrifying, though; rather, it was the enthusiasm of the listeners—especially the roaring choruses of the recurring slogan: *"Sieg Heil!"* ("Hail Victory!")

What kind of victory was this? What would happen to someone who dared to rebuke the hysterical speaker and the frenzied crowd with Saint Ireneus's words: *"Laus hominis Deus"* ("The glory of man is in God")? Or what if someone repeated Christ's words: "My peace I give you," *(Jn. 14:27)*, or, "This is my commandment: love one another"? *(Jn. 15:12)*.

The twentieth century was coming into its fifth decade at the time. It had already suffered through the First World War, which erupted in its second decade. Evidently man, "progressive" man, had come to believe in war. What does "progress" mean, though? Does it mean technical revolution? What kind, and at whose service? Military technical progress and organizational efficiency, mastered by one madman, caught the world unprepared. The world was incredulous and amazed; twentieth-century man was bewildered by his own creations. However, despite two world wars and other subsequent conflicts, man continues to channel his enormous technical progress into military machines. By no means is this for the service of man, though; it is not for his own good. Even for those who knew very little about the destructive potential of war, by the end of the twentieth century, no doubts remained about its vicious nature.

It should be enough to juxtapose our fantastic and incredibly expensive gains in technology with the hunger and illness suffered by great masses of poorer people. What kind of progress does this denote? To what end?

During the Second Vatican Council, from 1963 to 1965, a certain Professor Maurice Marois, a specialist in biology, did much toward developing contacts with bishops. He was present in his capacity as founder, in 1960, of the *Institut de la Vie* ("International Life Institute") based in Paris. His basic theme was the importance of recognizing Transcendental Authority in the world of science, and he spoke convincingly to many Council Fathers who represented individual Episcopal councils. Without recognizing such an Authority, without submitting to an ethical order, and without developing a sense of responsibility, he insisted that mankind, with its current scientific capabilities, is doomed to destruction—and not just mankind, but all life on earth. This belief, he said, is held by the scientists themselves—the discoverers who have come to wield powers unknown to date. Although this is the belief of men of science who are marked with a sense of responsibility, there also are many shortsighted scientists around who have amassed destructive powers capable of eradicating all life from the world several times over. We should not, therefore, only think of the problem of peacekeeping. We must also concentrate on the problem of saving life—a solution that man alone cannot guarantee. A scientist himself, Professor Marois understood this.

Simultaneously, especially related to the very basis of human existence, one-sided scientific progress jeopardizes human rights and values. As Pope John Paul II taught in his first encyclical:

> Are we of the twentieth century not convinced of the overpoweringly eloquent words of the Apostle of the Gentiles concerning the creation . . . (that) was 'subjected to futility'? Does not the previously unknown, immense progress which has taken place especially in the course of this century in the field of man's dominion over the world itself reveal—to a previously unknown degree—that manifold subjection to 'futility'? It is enough to recall certain phenomena, such as the threat of pollution of the natural environment in areas of rapid industrialization, or the armed conflicts continually breaking out over and over again . . . or the lack of respect for the life of the unborn. . . . Indeed there is already a real perceptible danger that, while man's dominion over the world of things is making enormous advances, he should lose the essential threads of his dominion and in various ways let his humanity be subjected to the world. . . . "[5]

The madman who wanted to create the Thousand Year Reich astonished the world with his military technology—and did so to the great affliction of mankind. We recall with great sadness the enormous number of people who died during the war he instigated. But were these the only people victimized by the mania of destruction? The war affected not only the victims, but also the perpetrators. In fact, all people are victims. Who will count them? Who will measure the extent of the damages wrought by this awful, deadly storm?

Some people say that it is necessary to forget. Is it not permissible to heal? Is it permissible to cease being vigilant? Who can pledge that the rule of such a diabolical ideology has passed—never to come back—and that no traces remain?[6]

The suggestion to forget once and for all is a very dangerous one. Forgetfulness is not the way to draw lessons from history. If it were, history would cease to be history, and culture, which includes historical awareness, would be seriously impaired.

It is important to be faithful to history—to European history and to world history. Include also the history of the Church, which is the history of the Mystical Body of Christ. This history is rich in martyrdoms, participations in Christ's own Cross, conversions, and the lives of the saints for the glory of God and the sustenance of man. Throughout history, the Church educates subsequent generations of the faithful. It draws on the legacy of centuries of experience, repeating *exempla trahunt* ("examples draw forth"), calling upon its treasury of saints. It is impossible to forget these saints: from the Apostles in the first century, to Saint Maximilian Kolbe, Edith Stein, and Bishop Michael Kozal in the twentieth. Furthermore, there is no way to depict their real lives without exposing the deeds of their persecutors and oppressors.

The Church is also familiar with the history of the astounding optimism revealed at the time when the greatest cruelty known to mankind was being wrought: "This day you will be with me in paradise," the Son of God promised from his Cross. *(Lk. 23:43).*

Therefore, being true to history is important.

Faithfulness to truth itself, however, is all the more important. Even when it becomes very difficult, it is still important to study it, and to endeavor to remember. "The truth shall set you free." *(Jn. 8:32)*. The Master who taught this also said: "All who are on the side of truth listen to my voice." *(Jn. 18:37)*. These are the prerequisites for a Civilization of Love. However, it is important not to omit the basic prerequisites of justice, including international justice.

Why fear truth? Why call for a complete forgetting? What are the motives? They are certainly not motives of culture or of faith. It is falsehood, not truth, which encumbers our consciences and infects the atmosphere of people's lives and communities. It also bears the burden of sadness. The truth that sets you free carries the final solution—just as in the camp chapel at Dachau, Christ, depicted in prisoner uniform hanging on the Cross, speaks of the Resurrection to come; just as right next door, in the Carmelite convent dedicated to the Most Precious Blood, perpetual prayers are raised and sacrifices offered in the spirit of joyful Christian hope.

Nevertheless, doubts may still linger in the minds of people, especially modern people. We are, after all, already tired, having witnessed all too many manifestations of evil, be they more distant, or closer at hand. Why should we recall these to memory? And if we do, which events should be given priority?

The answer is that there is a short and simple principle; namely, that we should never allow manifestations of evil to leave us resigned or indifferent.

At this point in our history, the manifestation of evil, and the extraordinary accumulation of it we encountered, fortunately failed to silence people's consciences completely. It did not manage to destroy the sacred, being rebuked in heed of Saint Paul's challenge: "Resist evil and conquer it with good." *(Rom. 12:21)*.

These inspired words reverberate throughout Poland even

today. They especially bore their mark in Saint Maximilian's *Niepokalanów* ("City of the Immaculate")—the community he founded near Warsaw. It was there that Pope John Paul II chose to repeat the challenge. In that bastion, built by a man of supposed defeat at the hands of a supposedly all-powerful evil, we found a man who was later given to us as a patron saint at the threshold of Poland's second millennium.

What immensity of evil he had conquered!

"Conquering evil . . . with good." *(Rom. 12:21)*. Such is the real meaning behind the history of Europe and the world. Such is the struggle that, however great the power of evil, knows but one end: the victory of the Civilization of Love.

This civilization struggles in its own particular way with every other civilization that transgresses its laws, though most of all with the one that stands opposed most definitely to Christ's commandment: "Love your enemies and do good to those who hate you." *(Lk. 6:27)*.

"They will despise you . . . on account of my name." *(Mk. 13:13)*. Did that apply to the Second World War also? Was it really for Christ's name's sake that battles were waged, and that suffering was endured? It is best when facts speak for themselves: in particular the modern-day *Acta Martyrum* ("Acts of the Martyrs").

Let me first reference a modern-day document: the memorandum of bishops and priests, past prisoners of Hitler's concentration camps, addressed to Pope John Paul II on April 29, 1982, prior to the canonization of Saint Maximilian Maria Kolbe. While this document refers to the saintly prisoner, it also speaks of all the rest, among whom he, Father Maximilian, was the first to be canonized. Let me, therefore, cite the full text:

Holy Father!
We write as bishops and priests, former prisoners of Hitler's

concentration camps, assembled in prayer in St. Joseph's sanctuary in Kalisz on April 29, 1982—the thirty-seventh anniversary of their rescue—in remembrance of our Brothers, who gave up their lives in concentration camps as priests of Christ, now as a much diminished group of survivors:

We wish to express to the vicar of Christ our deepest gratitude for his plans to number among the saints of the Church the blessed Maximilian Maria, priest and monk, who gave his life in the most horrendous extermination camp, Auschwitz, and did so in a great act of love in exchange for the father of a family when the man condemned to death exclaimed, "I am sorry to so orphan my children and wife." And we are so bold as to ask that the blessed Maximilian Maria Kolbe be elevated to the glory of the saints as a martyr.

Considering that, as priests and former Polish concentration camp prisoners, we have the obligation to present to Your Holiness the aforementioned request; we also ask that we may outline the motives behind our request. They are as follows:

1. The blessed Maximilian in his unique devotion and love for the Immaculate Virgin Mary wished, as he said, to be "ground into ash on behalf of the Immaculate Virgin Mary and for that ash to be blown around the world by the wind; only then would his sacrifice to the Immaculate be complete." This desire of his seems to have been inextricably linked to his desire for martyrdom, about which he thought of ever since his experience of the vision of the "two crowns" (the crown of purity and the crown of martyrdom). The spirituality of Father Maximilian was permeated by these choices (which, according to his mother's testimony, he made when he was ten years old) given that the future blessed said Mass by the altar on the grave of St. Peter in Rome on April 30, 1918, asking for the grace of martyrdom. This occurred again on December 25, 1918 in the church of St. Anastasia in Rome.

His desire to be ground into ash was carried out literally in the ferocious conditions of his cruel death in the concentration camp, and in the fate of his earthly remains after his death. The direct *causa movens* of his death was the family of a co-prisoner who was sentenced to death. Father Maximilian did not know the condemned man personally, but out of ten condemned men, he sacrificed his life for him, because as he said to his executioners: "He has a wife and children."

The fact that this priest-monk bore the greatest sacrifice on behalf of a family makes this martyrdom, in our present age of the family (as heralded in Your Holiness's speech to families on October 12, 1980), a great testimony to the harmony of vocations within the Church, as laid out in Your Holiness' teachings in the Apostolic Adhortation, "Familiaris Consortio."

2. It is our conviction as former camp prisoners (on which we agree with the prevailing opinion with no uncertainty), that the blessed Maximilian is a martyr for Christ:

(a) We will be so bold as to make reference to the wide variety of titles for the martyrdoms of Our Lord's saints known to the history of God's Church, of which St. Thomas Aquinas said: *"Potest esse quodcumque bonum humanum martyrii causa, secundum quod in Deum refertur"* (Aquinas II-II, q. 124, a. 8 ad 9);

(b) The first title for the martyrdom (although not the only one) of Father Maximilian is his heroic love: a love that matured through his entire life, and reached its ultimate maturity in the midst of all the hate that we also know from our firsthand experience. God clearly granted to Father Maximilian the gift of love, about which Christ said, "There is no greater love than this, that someone should lay down his life for his friends." *(Jn. 15:13)*.

(c) Furthermore, we wish to bear witness to the fact that Father Maximilian was in a concentration camp and suffered there as a Polish priest and monk. The whole history of Hitler's concentration camps attests to the fact that the number of Polish priests in the concentration camps was exceptionally high in proportion to the number of prisoners from other social strata and in proportion to the number of clergymen-prisoners from other ethnicities. The level of extreme suffering that was inflicted upon them was also exceptionally high, and it resulted in a large number of deaths.

Hence, the blessed Maximilian gave his life not only as a martyr of love, but also as a priest and monk who always fulfilled his calling with self-sacrifice up until his last days and death as a martyr. It was then that he realized the words of Christ: "Whoever will acknowledge me before others, I will acknowledge before my Father in Heaven." *(Mt. 10:32)*. All of this was examined with scientific accuracy and publicized—especially in the works of Fr. J.R. Bar, *Âmierç o. Maximiliana Kolbe* ("The Death of Fr. Maximilian Kolbe"); *Studia o Ojcu Maksymilianie Kolbe* ("Studies on Father Maximilian Kolbe"), Warsaw 1971, pgs. 5-59; and *Martyrologium polskiego duchowiefstwa rzymskokatolickiego pod okupacjà hitlerowskà 1939–1945* ("Martyrology of Roman-Catholic Polish clergy under Hitler's occupation 1939–1945"), Warsaw 1977, t. I – V.

Cardinal G. B. Montini, the later Pope Paul VI, wrote the preface for the book about Polish priests in concentration camps: *"E' un martirologio allora questo libro; e deve essere letto con la pacatezza e con la riverenza, con cui leggiamo le pagine sacre"* (Mons. F. Korszyfski "Un vescovo polacco a Dachau", Brescia 1963, preface, p. X).

3. Father Maximilian is a martyr in common belief. This belief prevails not only in Poland, but also, and this should be greatly emphasized, in Germany, where the blessed is officially worshiped as a martyr.

Thus, the canonization of Father Maximilian as a martyr would not only give renewed praise for the "Immaculate Virgin's madman," but it would also present this Polish priest, ground down into ash by love in the midst of a camp of hatred, as a representative of all those other brother priests who also gave up their lives for Christ as we testify. At the same time, it would show the Church and humanity the heroic sacrifice made by a priest on behalf of a family; this would have exceptional significance for our day, in accordance with the program in this area set forth in the Apostolic Adhortation "Familiaris Consortio."

For these reasons, we dare to humbly present our request to Your Holiness, and we implore Our Blessed Mother to aid you in your final decision as the Vicar of Christ by beseeching the enlightenment of the Holy Spirit and that she accept the uncounted sacrifices of other priest inmates who served as faithful witnesses of Christ, and whose lives were extinguished before our eyes, as contributions toward this first canonization of a concentration camp inmate.

Thus, it is important to be attentive and listen to witnesses. It is important to have their testimony before our eyes as long as the history of mankind lasts. There is no other way to understand and accept history in its full truth. However, it is legitimate to ask about those who are capable of telling us about such witnesses. Who is capable of giving evidence about their testimony, even if it concerns only a fragment of the harrowing struggles our century has seen?

In this testimony, the "fragment" is set in Hitler's concentration camps. It concerns what I experienced personally from the outbreak of the war to the day of my arrest, and then through to the day of my liberation and the end of the war. Everything took place between my time in the seminary at Wloclawek, up to my time in Dachau. The intermediate stages cover my imprisonment in Wloclawek, my internment in Lad nad Warta (a town on the River Warta), and my time in the Sachsenhausen concentration camp near Oranienburg.

3

The Attack

Spring and summer of 1939 were months that reverberated with optimism! There was much youthful hope to be found in the seminary students belonging to the oldest seminary in Poland—one that boasted many time-honored traditions. Our venerable Rector, Father Henryk Koczorowski, would warn us: "Do not wish for war. War is a great cataclysm." He was a man of great authority, so nobody questioned him. A moral theologian, he would often include considerations of our national characteristic strengths and weaknesses in his lectures. Besides, we were all well-grounded in our country's traditions and knew our patriotic duty. Over and above this, however, we were full of clerical ardor, and all around us we could see such slogans as: "Strong, united, ready!"

Who could know that we were neither strong, nor ready? We were indeed united, though; united in patriotism forged by the history we knew, and in an ever-present patriotism, strong within us however much it was tested, and perhaps even strongest in times of trial.

We never anticipated the cataclysm that was about to befall us. The populace was getting ready for war—ourselves included. The leading concern in Poland was that of defense against air attacks. It was also emphasized that the enemy might use poison gas. (The Second World War was to begin where the First ended). The people were very generous in giving for the cause of the country's defense; everyone was sacrificing much for the war effort.

Our students were among the representatives of various classes and trades who proudly stood next to the donated military equipment exhibited on Dabrowski square. The elated, yet clouded and highly emotional, atmosphere was cogently captured by the command: "March!" which was transmitted over the radio when the General in Command ordered the occupation of Zaolzie.

We were very attentive to the diplomatic efforts expended by our politicians on the international scene (they could not be sure of our trust, though they were still seen as "ours"). We eagerly followed any news of international agreements, as well as communiqués on the ominous activities of Hitler in Austria and Czechoslovakia. The ripples from those undertakings were directed against us, and were, therefore, particularly repulsive. They took the form of a series of programs from Gleiwitz entitled, "Isn't It Amazing?"[7] Soon, a whole tornado of propaganda swirled around us. (From now on, will it ever be possible to view the words "agitation" and "propaganda" in a positive light? Already in those early days we were witnesses to an inhuman hypothesis being carried out with pertinacity, and we saw how people could be talked into anything!)

We were well informed of events in the Third Reich, particularly thanks to Joseph Kisielewski's book, *The Earth Is Collecting Ashes.*[8] The book was informative, but alarming. Somehow, I have managed to remember one particular phrase from the book: "Szczecin is Berlin's courtyard." It is worthwhile to pause at one chapter's title: "Berlin to Szczecin—90 minutes." Sixty years later, in the 1990s, the wait at the frontier on the route between Szczecin and Berlin was alone, seldom shorter than ninety minutes.

Let us return to 1939—the time of anticipation. What came upon us, came suddenly. War was not declared; we were simply attacked. Compared to what we had anticipated, the actual attack differed in every way. It was attack and annihilation!

However, one thing remained set: before the holiday, we were told that in the event of war we were to return to the seminary. Thus, we had to go back. The route from Zloczew to Wloclawek was always a long one, but now it had become almost impossible. The longest interruption of the journey was in Kutno. The enemy knew it was a crucial connection point for several communication routes, so the air raids there were relentless. We embarked on trains only to disembark again. At one point I found myself in the company of several army officers. Dressed in their elegant uniforms, their behavior was extremely serene, and understandably so. On several occasions, individuals would turn to me and ask for the Sacrament of Penance. Their colleagues would then retort: "Do not agree to his request; he's losing courage!" What a misunderstanding! I endeavored to explain and to call in a priest, the army chaplain, for the individual who asked. I advised the others to seize the opportunity as well, saying that to fight with a pure heart is a condition of true courage, and that such was the tradition of Polish arms-bearing, and the underpinning of all Polish victories in centuries past.

Bombs were falling unabated from planes that seemed to command the Polish skies, and a powerful army stormed across borders via multiple routes, overrunning the land. It turned out that there was no poison gas, but there certainly was terror and panic.

Surrender? No. Thankfully, we received encouraging news of heroic battles and resistance. Meanwhile, however, enemies were becoming the lords of the skies over the whole country—especially above the capital. How was it possible to give credence to such a catastrophe? A vast number of conjectures arose, including one that all of our planes had flown off to bomb Berlin and level it to the ground.

Disorientation prevailed. The Bishop of Chelm, Stanislaw Wojciech Okoniewskich, visited Wloclawek just prior to the exodus of our seminarians. He and our own Bishop, Karol Radonski, agreed that we should follow the example of our government and cross Poland's southern frontier. Needless to say, this was only to be for the time being. The group of elder seminarians, however, myself included, was told to make its way to Lublin. There we expected that we would be able to continue our studies in peace at the Catholic University of Lublin, which was closely affiliated with the major seminary in Wloclawek. Therefore, we began making preparations for our departure.

Meanwhile, debates among the seniors of the seminary continued. The constant discussions were quickly ended, however, by Bishop Michael Kozal. He was a newcomer from Gniezno, and was an auxiliary bishop consecrated for the diocese of Wloclawek only a few days before the outbreak of the war. We knew him, but only superficially. He spoke little, so we could not get to know him from his words, but he proved to be very active. He visited all of the churches in Wloclawek and heard confessions at each of them. Shortly after, the diocesan bishop departed and Bishop Kozal was left alone. From then on, he had to shoulder all of the responsibilities for his diocese without assistance, and as it turned out, he had to do this for longer than anyone anticipated, and in circumstances no one could have foreseen.

In accordance with our instructions, we made our way in the direction of Warsaw and Lublin. We reached Warsaw on the last day of its heroic defense. Yet, even though the city had surrendered, at that time we nevertheless failed to grasp that the battle had not just been in defense of Warsaw, but that Poland's entire struggle for independence was coming to an end. We were incredulous. We couldn't have been defeated yet! Surely we hadn't fallen!

Our journey witnessed roads full of horse-drawn carriages and refugees trying to escape on foot with their families and possessions. Cars stood abandoned on the roadside, gas tanks empty, useless for lack of fuel. Where were all these people from, and where were they going? Surely they were trying to escape from some dreadful danger, but where to? Where was it safe? They traveled while it was safest, under the cover of night. But this, too, was coming to an end. No place was safe any longer, and no time was better than any other. The roads were soon lit up at night by bomber-planes that bombed indiscriminately. It was all a prelude of things to come.

None of our expectations came to be fulfilled, and our last vestiges of hope were slowly being extinguished. In Warsaw, I happened to meet a friend who was now wearing an officer's uniform on an army motorcycle. I risked saying: "I hope we soon meet in the joy and celebration of victory." He answered: "In joy and celebration outside of Warsaw!" Unfortunately, he was not being cynical. The truth was borne out in events that followed one another with blinding speed: the terrible attack; the heroic defense; and ultimately, the capital's capitulation. The awful screams: "They're coming!" gave way to the subsequent silence. The enemy had arrived.

The enemy arrived in order to more and more indiscriminately carry out the intentions of its attack: the extermination of the nation. That was the plan. First, there was the scheme which had already been commenced for extermination of the Jewish people. Now, the enemy was after the Polish. *Ausradieren!* ("Annihilation!")—such was the whim of the Nazi Commander in Chief; such was his command.

The extermination project was not only a scheme of hatred, but also one of scorn and contempt. Where did it all come from? Had all the worst precedents of history been drawn out, going back to the skirmishes against Western Slavs in the days of the Carolingian empire? Was it some kind of historical piling-together of evil, symbolized by the broken cross: the swastika? But it all had to be defeated. Good had to survive. Christianity, after all, had been introduced to Poland with the country's baptism almost 1,000 years previously. Who could know that this country of ours would suffer such viscious aggression from its neighbors throughout the twentieth century? The unquenched glow of the Jasna Góra Monastery in Czestochowa continued to shine forth. The enemy was forced to recognize that fact, and not for the first time in our country's history.

We now had to make our way back from fallen Warsaw to Wloclawek. Our first means of transportation was a ship endeavoring to navigate the Vistula River. En route, we encountered several exploded bridges, and allegedly mines, as well. Nevertheless, we eventually made it. It was now October, but how different the seminary's prospects were this time. It was as if it were in a coma. It would probably wake up; at least that is what we thought. The bishop sought permission from the authorities to attempt to bring it back to life, so that it could return to its work.

4

The Gate Slammed Shut Behind Us

The night of occupation enveloping Wloclawek was progressively darkening. The town was given the name Leslau, a name unheard of by any of its inhabitants, and a new daily newspaper began to come out, called the *Leslauer Bote*. Everything for the new Leslau had been prepared in advance with precision.

Systematic arrests ensued. In the seminary, alongside the prefects, the priest lecturers, who were also teachers at the Pius X Lycée, were taken first. These included Father Michael Morawski, a historian and fellow of the University of Stefan Batory in Vilnius, Father Anthony Pawlak, a pedagogue, Father Mieczyslaw Chwilowicz, a mathematician and the ex-director of the seminary, and Father Faustyn Stefanczyk, a classical philologist. The superiors then instructed Father Professor Stefan Wyszynski, editor-in-chief of *The Priestly Athenaeum* to leave as well. Officers of the *Wermacht* ("the German Nazi Army," renowned for its discipline) were taking over more and more of the seminary's premises, and they would be sure to take over any free rooms immediately; thus, before his departure, Father Professor asked me to take over his flat in the hope of rescuing the library. However, I failed to rescue the books. Our turn to be arrested arrived, and I was taken along with two other alumni who joined me at the expressed wish of the Father Professor.

Bishop Kozal, not discouraged by anything, continued his ardent efforts to obtain permission to reopen the seminary, and he kept our superiors informed of the course of his efforts. His negotiations proved to be very difficult. "I cannot recognize these Germans," the Bishop commented. "They're so different from the ones I once knew."

Two feasts passed by: Christ the King and All Saints—both so ceremoniously celebrated year-in and year-out in the cathedral. This year, however, the place resounded with emptiness. These were the only pontifical Masses that this eminent bishop was ever to celebrate. I had the honor of assisting him as a sub-deacon on both occasions. (I had not yet been ordained to the priesthood, only to the diaconate.)

On November 7, 1939, we were told that the efforts of our bishop had finally come to fruition, and that the occupying authorities had allowed the seminary to resume its work the following day. But that unforgettable day, November 7, was not over yet. The long autumn evening of that day was still before us—so long, and so memorable. It was the evening of the arrest of all of the seminary's professors and students.

The *Schutzstaffel* (SS) officers' knowledge of the seminary's layout was excellent. The Wermacht had been stationed here for weeks, and not in vain. Only one man, Father Ignacy Rudzinski, the seminary's spiritual director, escaped arrest, and he did so only through sheer chance. As seminarians, we were included in the operation. Father Stefan Wyszynski's quarters were among the first to be evacuated. Everything happened in relative peace and quiet, but fear plagued us. This was the first time I had been arrested in my life, and the fear was also the first such fear I had ever experienced. It was paralyzing. My prison hand-luggage was ready. I had only removed some small items in the last few days, meaning to put them back when necessary, but I did not repack again. I was as if in shock. In silence, it being almost nighttime, we were rounded up on the street in front of the seminary by guards of the new order who appeared to arise from nowhere. A small escort leading Bishop Kozal joined us. Those were his last steps on the streets of Wloclawek, and were the last steps there for a number of others, as well. The road was not long: Seminary Street; past Saint Witalis' Church; Karnkowski Street; and then into the prison grounds. I do not remember whether the prison gates were opened loudly, but to this day, I can hear the dull bang of their shutting all too well, and I still shudder at its ominous meaning.

They led all of us—apart from the bishop—through the prison courtyard and around the buildings' corners into quite a large cell. It was apparent from the outset that it had once been a chapel. There was an altar in the center and liturgical implements stood by. There was nothing that could humanly enable us to carry out the command: "Everybody sleep!" There was only just about enough room on the floor for everyone to lay down, squeezed in among each other. We placed shoes, boots, or small bundles under our heads. It was not possible to leave the room at night, according to prison rules.

Our group was forty-three all told: priest-lecturers and seminary tutors, curia clergy, parish priests, and clerics. There were elderly men among us, as well. All of the priests in Wloclawek had not yet been arrested; a few remained free. The arrests were carried out in stages, determined by a code known only to the all-powerful *Geheime Staatspolizei* ("Gestapo—the Nazi Secret State Police"). One thing, however, became more and more clear: they had undertaken the task of the elimination of all Polish Catholic clergy.

Before this was made incontrovertibly clear, though, borne out by the sheer number arrested and in the special torments devised against the clergy, we could already begin to get the picture in the first hours of our internment in the Wloclawek prison. The prison became increasingly full, and executions were being carried out! The arrests concerned people known to the Gestapo by name. Our personal details, however, were not taken down until we were in the prison cell, even though they were already partly known because the Gestapo had diocesan lists at their disposal. It was commonly said in the outside world that, to the occupier, the position of Polish clergy was politically inimical. This would explain the arrests. Hitler's propaganda machine had evidently been successful here. However, such a decidedly politically inimical position was common to the whole nation. Thus, the arrests were aimed in general, at the influential layers of society; i.e., the educated classes and those who, as priests, held particularly strong influence among the people, and bore responsibility for the spiritual values they espoused. Neither my friends nor I would ever get involved in politics, but all of us, together with the more aged priests of Wloclawek, were perceived as dangerous through our very belonging to the clerical state. The *Warthegau* ("administration of occupied Polish territory") just simply had no use for any of us, neither as laborers nor as soldiers. We were first given the label *Schützhäftling* ("concentration-camp prisoner charged with the role of prefect over other prisoners"), and it was only later that we were asked for our names and surnames.

"Schützhäftling!" A good hearted, rather naïve prison governor endeavored to explain to us the whole structure of deception: "You have been arrested a few days prior to November 11, because that day marks a national feast of yours. It was necessary to take you under our guard so that you do not get hurt by your fellow people who are angry with you." Who thought that up? Who could believe it? Our prison governor believed it, and it probably made it easier for him to carry out his work. The whole of society was straight-jacketed into such a structure of deception! We would later come across this more than once.

Besides deception, there was also theft. It was announced to us that we were to hand in all of our money, down to the last penny, but that it would all be noted down in order to be returned later, "given that we comprised a society of honest people." Of course, all of the money was gone forever. Nobody, however, gave it any thought because of all of the other events that were happening, which preoccupied our minds.

We tidied up our overcrowded cell, introducing discipline and order, and our seniors set a daily prison timetable. Efforts were made to enable us to offer the Holy Mass, and we soon became a united community despite our age differences. Time was set aside for prayer, study, talks, meals, and conversation. The talks and conversations concerned selected theological questions. Memories from the history of the Wloclawek diocese and our seminary also were shared, and our seminary traditions were recalled. The tragic political situation of Poland kept coming up in conversation, as well. Study, including the learning of languages, became feasible thanks to books brought in to us from the outside. Discussions among the younger clerics came to revolve more and more around prospects for change. Apparently the Germans had built some concentration camps—why weren't they taking us there? Nobody had any idea of the dreadfulness of such a prospect.

At first, the prison authorities failed to provide us any meals, so we were indebted to a few very generous nuns who managed to talk the prison guards into passing on food they supplied. The good sisters also sent us much more, including news. There was no way we could have done without their secret messages.

What about prayer in prison? After our morning wakeup call and some necessary setting of things in order, we would line up in the corridor and commence meditation and quiet prayer as we were led off in silence. I remember this very clearly—the scene of this procession of prisoners engrossed in prayer is still vivid before my eyes to this day.

One of the Gestapo dignitaries granted us permission for a weekly Sunday Mass to be offered by our bishop. Half an hour was allocated to it. The guards escorted Bishop Kozal to us at the given hour. He would first ask Monsignor Anthony Borowski to hear his confession, and then straightaway he would say Mass. No words of conversation were exchanged—our state of recollection and the shortage of time did not allow it. At least we could see our bishop and participate in the Holy Mass offered up by him, though. That, in itself, meant a lot. We were aware that Bishop Kozal was being kept in total isolation on a cement floor in a basement cell. The conditions he was kept in were beginning to take their toll. Week by week, we could observe that he was finding it more difficult to walk, and in particular, to kneel.

The day arrived, a Sunday, when the governorship of the prison was taken over by a more unyielding officer—one with a heart of stone. This new officer could not even contemplate a prisoner's friendly face. Our rector, the good-natured Father Franciszek Korszynski, would have had to pay dearly for one such smile he had given, if somebody had not intervened on the spot to explain its meaning in proficient German.

On one occasion, this officer entered our chapel-cell during Mass, just after the consecration, and insisting that the thirty minutes were over, started shouting: *Bischof raus!* ("Bishop out!") Seeing that the celebrant's pose did not change, he raised his voice even more and began to make his way toward the altar. Dread passed among us. We would say later that it seemed that the martyrdom of Saint Stanislaus at Skalka[9] was about to be re-enacted. The priests closest to the altar advised the bishop to consume the

Sacred Species himself and finish the Mass, and this course of action was adopted. The bishop was escorted away immediately.

What was Bishop Kozal experiencing? A few weeks later he was once more allowed to meet us all for a short while during Christmas Eve. By then, we were all divided among different cells and provided with straw sleeping mats, so it was an occasion for us all to come together again. The bishop spoke to us concisely, emphasizing words from the Breviary: *Crastina die delebitur iniquitas terrae!* ("Tomorrow the wickedness of the world shall be destroyed!") He was not one to be deceived. He was a realist, and was aware of the whole terrible situation; but above all, he was a realist of faith.

As for us, we now had a completely different world to contend with. In particular, feast days gave occasion for the representatives of the Reich, officers of various ranks, to come and visit the "zoological exhibits" which we, as prisoners, had become. That was how they looked upon us and how they behaved. How distant one human being can become from another! After all, it was not what we wanted. We did nothing to make it that way. When the visitors entered, we would all freeze at the command: *Achtung!* ("Attention!") We had to stand at attention—that was the position due toward the authorities; it was a position that simultaneously humiliated us, and fed the pride of our "lords."

Despite all the darkness, however, there were rays of heroism which did not fail to brighten our days. A younger colleague of ours, Bronislaw Kostkowski, comes to mind. His parents, who lived in Bydgoszcz (a city quelled with great bloodshed right at the beginning of the war), managed, with persistent effort, to obtain his freedom. Bronislaw was informed that he would be set free under one condition: he would have to renounce any thoughts of the priesthood. His unhesitating response was, "No." He informed us of this on his return to the cell. We did not look upon him then as a hero, though he was one for certain. He later died in Dachau as a seminarian, maintaining his faithfulness toward the priesthood to which he aspired. More later joined him, including my personal friend, Stanislaw Grzesitowski, who also could have escaped his terrible fate in the camp if only he had agreed to declare that he would not be a priest.

There were more such examples, but I must return to the chronological account of events.

January brought a total changeover in its wake. We were to be transported, but where to? No one knew. Two Lorries covered in canvas drove us out of the prison gates. Where to? The question increasingly began to haunt us. There were only two possible directions: either that of Warsaw, toward the so-called General Government; or that of Poznan, which denoted darkness beyond . . . We soon realized that we were being taken in the direction of Poznan.

The frost was biting, but we were more chilled to the bone by the bleak prospect of our circumstances, rather than by the cold weather. Bishop Kozal was with us; he was worried, but calm. The journey through the snow lasted a very long time. Then, suddenly, we came to our first stop at Slupiec. We had traveled far already.

After a short break, we continued toward Poznan. Cars were stopping all around us, unable to pass through the snow drifts. The frosty wind blew over us as we were thrown off the Lorries to dig a way out through the snow. How were we to manage it? Somehow we did. That stage of our journey finally ended, and we arrived at the well-lit Salesian monastery in Lad n. Warta.

5

Where Important Decisions Were Made

Far-reaching events would later unfold in the Salesian monastery in Lad n. Warta. Singular decisions with unforeseeable consequences would later be made, but so far, the monastery was a place of respite: light, warm, humane, and even godly. The contrast between this institution and our previous prison was great. There were real people here, and no one else. A real human being was responsible for us—a Silesian priest, who was the institution's so-called director. He was responsible for us, but he also had his own personal safety and life to answer for. We respected his position. Furthermore, the local people showed us much good will, including the priests who, for the time being, were still able to enjoy freedom.

Everything had a given order. We had to do the cleaning, study, and take duty shifts in the church and in the refectory. While the atmosphere was one of contemplation, there were moments for recreation, and unlimited time to give service to God in the beautiful, albeit cold, church.

Bishop Kozal continued to set the tone of the place. He interfered little, but took a discreet interest in our lives. We found out that he was learning Italian, among his other occupations. When he discovered that one of us was proficient in the language, he asked him for conversation sessions during his walks in the garden.

Bishop Kozal would always offer Holy Mass at the main altar, and every day he would spend several hours alone in prayer in the church. We soon came to notice that it was becoming more and more difficult for him to kneel, yet we observed how long he spent kneeling in prayer during the day. He could have prayed in his own room, which clearly would be the indicated course of action taking into account his rheumatism and the cold temperature of the otherwise wonderful sanctuary. He preferred, however, to be close to the Most Holy Sacrament, and so he kept vigil, humble, and unmoved. The bishop continued to kneel. . . .

The depths of intercommunication between the Hidden God and an individual human person will always largely remain a secret to us. However, at a later date, part of the veil of intimacy came to be lifted for us. During this time, in the Lad church, the bishop made a prodigious decision: this quiet and great man resolved to give his life to God. It was still a young life, one that had just embarked on its Episcopal mission. He had not yet ordained any priests; he had never celebrated a pontifical High Mass in freedom; he had never experienced crowds of the faithful. Nevertheless, he offered the sacrifice, and received some confirmation that it had been accepted. He was convinced of this—as he would confide to us later, when the sacrifice was about to be completed.

What had been his motive? The impulses of grace and man's responses to them remain in the realm of mystery. I can only witness to what I saw myself. At lunchtime one day, as the bishop was about to descend from the floor where he had his room to the ground floor, he was surrounded by a group of us, and we could observe his reaction to the news that the Western front had broken down. His posture stiffened, but the announcement failed to overcome him. That is not to say that he was already broken. The surprise was a painful one. He could see anew what a great price would have to be paid to rescue Poland and the Church from the deluge.

As seminarians, we took no part in the negotiations that ensued from the proposal that Bishop Kozal take over the Episcopal See of Lublin. (These events have already been reported elsewhere.) In these, as in all future decisions, the Bishop showed great clarity of thought.

Two such decisions turned out to be of particular bearing.

The first decision concerned priestly ordinations. At this point, the eldest group of seminarians had taken advantage of the relatively peaceful conditions at Lad, and had passed all of the necessary pre-examinations. They were admitted to the final exam—the *rigorosum* ("rigorous"). The students who remained free also were admitted. The preparation was thorough, and the panel-type examination was taken very seriously. Everyone passed. The bishop, sitting at the head of the examining panel at my exam in pastoral theology, intervened to correct a common but imprecise idea of what denotes a "good parish." Clearly, having been a teacher for many years, he was still sensitive to the pastoral aspect of the priestly mission. This had best been borne out in the few weeks of his Episcopal service in Wloclawek in wartime conditions. It also was proved by his resolve to remain faithful to his pastoral mission, which will be discussed in more detail later.

During the subsequent celebrations, we received Bishop Kozal's announcement that he was unable, despite all the happily completed preparations, to ordain us. The Church demands that candidates for the priesthood be fully free. We lacked such freedom, since, as co-prisoners, we were necessarily tied by the force of circumstance to our tutors and to our bishop.

Apparently, his decision was completely independent. Needless to say, it took us by surprise. However, in the long run, it would turn out to be the right one. The legitimate defense of the principle of freedom by the Church was reason enough. Later on, the decision was further validated by the fact that one of our colleagues eventually turned away from his aspirations to the priesthood.

Moreover, it also should be kept in mind that some aspects of the bishop's decision demanded his own personal sacrifice, as well.

The first such aspect—a very important one for the celebrant of ordinations—was that Bishop Kozal had never before ordained priests. Here, by his own decision, he moved that prospect even further away. His renouncement was all the more marked in that he authorized the seminarians who remained in freedom to seek ordination at the hands of other bishops.

The second compounding difficulty came from the fact that the bishop expected that we would be transported to some concentration camp where, according to his own words, he foresaw that his "seminarians would suffer for the priesthood to which they had not yet been admitted."

Another one of Bishop Kozal's decisions concerned his steadfastness with regard to his pastoral mission. It happened at one point in the course of the summer when quite a high-ranking Gestapo representative arrived and announced to us that each prisoner had the right to declare his wish to travel to the areas controlled by the General Government. They insisted that the fulfillment of such a desire would be guaranteed. As for those who wished to stay, however, no decisions had yet been made.

Difficult discussions ensued. The bishop announced that his priests could legitimately agree to leave and make their way to the area of the General Government, with the exception of those who performed pastoral duties in the wake of arrest. They, he said, would continue to serve before God, the churches, and the faithful who had been entrusted to their care.

Closely following this decision came another—a worthy decision made by our tutors and professors. (Their surnames ought to be made known—their priestly and patriotic stature, and their exemplary and generous lives are a priceless legacy and heritage, and are models for us to follow. As for the present, however, my memories of them are necessarily very limited, even though the lives of each one would deserve separate monographs.[10]) The decision our professors made was as follows: "We will all stay in Lad so long as even one of our students remains here."

Most of us stayed, and all of them stayed. The last I remember as living was Monsignor Franciszek Maczynski, who was then serving as rector of the Polish Institute in Rome. All of them went through the torments of the concentration camp, and some would stay there forever.

Witnesses indeed.

Like Bronislaw Kostkowski.

Like all who heeded Bishop Kozal's decision, occasionally buckling under the yoke of obedience.

Like the bishop himself—witnesses!

6

Into the Unknown

August 26, 1940, commenced as usual: morning prayers, meditation, and Holy Mass. Indeed, a series of Masses was offered one right after another, because the number of priests had increased markedly from the time of our imprisonment in Wloclawek and the arrests of diocesan and monastic clergy alike. As students, we served several Masses each day. Therefore, it was not surprising that the alarm informing us of the arrival of the Gestapo with transport vans found me at the Altar of the Holy Cross, in the right nave of the Church, serving at the seventh consecutive Holy Mass that morning.

We all assembled in the historic Abbot's Hall. The sorting commenced: eight of the elder priests were separated away, with Bishop Kozal among them. (We thought this was because his office merited respect and heed was being taken of his age. A few months later, though, we found out how wrong we were.) They ordered the rest of us to prepare for departure within a few minutes.

Once again, we all fell prey to that same feeling we experienced on November 7: a paralyzing fear. Perhaps we had an intuition. It was difficult to keep our wits about us. All of a sudden we were to make preparations for a journey. Where? Why? What would happen to us? Out of necessity, the preparations were short and confused.

We were loaded tightly so that we would fit in together with our luggage (which would prove to be only a hindrance.) Once again we became non-humans. Our destination was Szczyglin, a small town in the Poznan district, which was a collection point for priests transported from all districts of the Warthegau. The whole process lasted three days. Once, while we stood in file, someone was set free.

These are very distant memories, but others are more distinct.

Two priests were found to be missing from our transport from Lad. The Gestapo was surprised and furious. Searches were made, but to no avail. Will we have to pay for this? The thought came to us, but thankfully nothing was done. It was not camp yet, and it would prove to be different there.

Another very vivid memory of mine was when we were again ordered to relinquish all of our money. This was forced upon us with awful screams and a hateful grimace by a young SS man who insisted on being terrible toward us. He was definitely in the mold of the stone-hearted prison governor at Wloclawek, and his behavior was but another foretaste of what awaited us at camp. The officers screamed so hideously and wanted to hate us so dreadfully! It can be said that the camps consisted of one great scream, and that they were indeed, places of concentrated hatred.

Can more be said of these camps? Yes—more has to be said. In truth, it is difficult to imagine a worse reality devised by man, but it is not right to stop at generalizations. Above all, it is important to underline that this plethora, this overabundance, of evil still did not comprise the full reality. It represented but a semblance of reality. The camps were manifestations of evil where the deficiency of good resounded with the cry: "Conquer evil with good. . . ."

The rest of our journey to camp was by train. In the first days after our arrest, we found it incredible that we were denied any information about what awaited us. Our destinies were in the hands of men who not only usurped the total right to dispose of our freedom, but also the sole right to know how they planned to dispose of it. The only thing becoming more and more evident was that they were going to do so with more and more cruelty and blatancy.

Finally, we arrived in Berlin. We were duly assembled at the *Alexanderplatz* ("a large, open square in Berlin") in clerical garb—our cassocks. The glances and taunts thrown at us by passers-by evidenced disregard and contempt, which were the fruits of the efficient propaganda machine. The very fact that we were in cassocks already gave witness, and the fact that we were Polish clergy increased the disrespect.

After the war the famous Father Bernard Lichtenberg would make a point of walking the streets of Berlin in precisely such dress. Years later, in 1986, one of us from this group that had been welcomed in such an unfriendly way, was invited to visit Berlin's Saint Hedwig Cathedral in an official capacity. His welcome then was both formal and very friendly. Was this a meeting in a new and different epoch? How much we had yearned for things to turn around that way! It was certainly a meeting with disciples of a different school: that of Christ. If only this school could finally encompass all human hearts!

We were in Berlin, and once again there were gates—as if reminding us of those first gates in Wloclawek. Past the gates: Hell! There were wild screams of hatred, violent dragging of the elder priests by their cassocks out of the high vans, beatings with sticks snatched from the passers-by, and the bellowing of *"Los! Los!"* ("Hurry! Hurry!") that was later relentless.

They were driving a herd, not people, into the bathhouse. Next to me was an elder priest, Father Mateusz Grabowski, who was the parish priest from Dab nad Nera. I wondered how long he would last because he was already panting very heavily.

"Take everything off!" Our hair was cut, and we were shaved and bathed. Over the camp gates, we heard, *"Sauberkeit ist gesundheit"* ("Cleanliness is health") and *"Arbeit macht frei!"* ("Work sets you free!"). This "Sauberkeit" and "Arbeit" were deceptive, though; not only because they did not mean freedom at all, but also because such freedom no longer existed.

The camp was full of vermin and pests, despite all of the fumigation measures, which included the degrading *Lauskontrolle* ("lice control"). Lice were one of the camp plagues, were later a vector of typhoid fever, and were always a humiliating torment—although they took a much less prominent place among the other torture procedures, which constantly threatened life. It is not true that a person can get used to anything. Even now, after so many decades, when I sit down on benches in the French Metro stations I have to look around to make sure there is no danger.

Sauberkeit, like everything else in the camp according to the authorities' assumptions, became an inhuman phenomenon and a torture. The floors, the so-called *Sztuby,* had to shine, so not only were they polished until perfect through *Stubendiest* ("barracks management"), but we also had to walk on them with the utmost care, almost with reverence, and in our rag-socks of course. As soon as we returned from work, we would take off our *pantines* on the porch. Pantines were a special type of camp footwear: wooden underneath, with the top consisting of a bit of cloth held by a piece of string. It was possible to learn to walk in these, though it was sometimes quite an art, especially in the snow. After use, the pantines had to be washed in water and subsequently set in an even row on a shelf. Any lack of precision, even if only apparent, could and often did result in heavy punishment.

Sauberkeit and *Ordnung*—cleanliness and orderliness—became the utmost of tortures during *Bettenbau* ("the making of one's bed according to strict rules"). It was not just making the beds; rather, it was building them. The sleeping mat, blanket, and small straw pillow had to be made even with their edges stiff. Furthermore, everything had to be exactly in line with the neighboring beds. Our cupboards were constantly checked to make sure everything was in its place, as if called to attention. This included a camp set of polished eating implements. The worst item was the often-used aluminum bowl. One could and had to eat the soup (the only meal ever provided in camp) quickly; however, to wash and polish the bowl quickly was impossible. Nevertheless, it still had to be polished to a shine.

False gods were set up. They were many in number, and were untouchable, guarded by thugs. The camp gods were particularly malignant. Their creators, likewise, were cruel. Are not humans always devising new gods? In camp, they were very arrogant, having been taught in their *Ordensburgs* ("training schools for Nazi leaders") how to be cruel to other men, and that it is shameful to ever kneel.

Meanwhile, we were continuously subjected to the Sauberkeit procedures, and treated like a herd of cattle. There was no chance for any privacy—not in the bath-house; not at any moment of camp life. It was this way until the end. In the meantime, we were given some rags for underclothes and some striped overalls (the camp uniform), and were rushed off once again.

The thought came irresistibly: Satan reigns here. A few years after the war, I was told of a discussion during which the famous psychologist, Jung, asked the speaker: "If there is no Satan, how can you explain concentration camps?"

This time, we were being rushed to our block, as the camp jargon had it. Here we came across another written announcement:

Im Lager nur Laufschritt ("Only brisk walking is allowed in camp"). This was yet another aberration contrary to human nature and rights: we were only allowed to run. It was more than an aberration, however; it was meant to add to the intentional humiliation of slave-prisoners. Did such an idea ever find ground in the old days of slavery? Such devices of oppression, together with many, many others, had probably never before been known to mankind.

That is how we encountered the bitter adventure of travel into the unknown. . . But no, it turned out not to be bitter in its inner meaning. It turned out to be a grace—a momentous grace.

Packed into a camp hall, crowded together like cattle, we had to listen to our first lecture on camp discipline. Among the points emphasized was one that I remember to this day: ". . . is the son of Death." I suppose it was some kind of warning that we should not approach the electric fences. However, a few moments later we came to be convinced that everything there was loaded with death and had a deadly potential.

It took but a few days for the first victims of our transport to depart from among us. They were not electrocuted, but were taken victim by the cold September mornings which the prison rags failed to keep at bay. What would happen in December and January? There was no time for despair or lamentation, though, and there was still the possibility of hardening ourselves against the cold with frosty water—one thing that was available to us in abundance. The cold, nevertheless, would always remain one of the greatest perils of camp.

Next we were led to the camp registration board. The procedure was exact and lasted a long time. There were several clerks, and I was assigned to one of the young German prisoners. He was a tall man, decisive and calm, and behind his glasses his eyes were friendly and lit up when I told him I was a seminarian. "And I," he said, "I'm a deacon. My name is Karl Leisner."

I could not have suspected at the time that one day I would be called to witness for the cause of his beatification.

I was given number 29 655: a significant event that must be commented on.

The number was all-important. In all concentration camps, it was not the person that counted—only the number. The number had to report whenever called upon: *"Nummer . . . meldet sich gehorsamst zur Stalle!"* ("Number . . . obediently come forward!") Behind the prison gates, a number was enough for the authorities.

The number was important, but so was the count. We were continuously counted. When the count was right, we were asked about our numbers. When the count was short, a grim drama commenced. In Auschwitz, this was the backdrop of the heroic gesture of prisoner number 16 670, Father Kolbe. He had been asked about his number when he made the offer to take the place of another prisoner marked for the starvation bunkers. He was then asked, *"Wer bist Du?"* ("Who are you?") Thus, his humanity tore through in an extraordinary way, overcoming the camp's number dialectic. The human person, in entering into the orbit of such great dehumanizing forces, need not subject himself entirely after all.

The number was, therefore, important to the individual prisoner as a challenge: that the person who was treated like a number not become a number. Saint Maximilian Kolbe, number 16 670, is now a holy martyr. He is the patron of human dignity, and was salvaged at the price of his life through God's grace. His dignity was salvaged in many others; salvaged, and even elevated to its heights.

We rapidly discovered much about our concentration camp (what an inadequate label!). We found out later that every camp was the same; only the type of work differed—as in the awful quarries of Gusen or Mauthausen, for instance. But work was meant as torture everywhere. We shivered when, in Sachsenhausen, they begin to shout: *"Freiwillige vor!"* ("Volunteers come forward!") We "volunteers" were responsible for carrying cut pine logs in from the nearby forest, for toting bricks piled onto our bare hands and chests (in the cold!), and for carrying freshly dug-out roots that pierced our shoulders through with moisture. However, it was not the type of work alone that was awful: later, in Dachau, they would turn shoveling snow, a task that could very well be both healthy and pleasant, into torment. Everything that was human was distorted into a diabolical grimace of hatred.

Our first morning brought us to a task that remained the duty of the clergy until the end: distributing kettle drums from the kitchen throughout the entire camp. The weight was awful, but we grew used to it. Physical exertion requires exercise—for which we had ample opportunity as long as our strength held out.

Finally, hunger was an integral part of the camp program. We received a portion of thick soup, a camp specialty (later we became aware that it consisted of turnips, carrots, and cabbage in rotation) that was impossible to swallow all in one go. Then we noticed that in our neighboring block, which also turned out to be one of clergy from Wloclawek, our friends were all emaciated. They sent us signs of greeting from their windows, and then, seeing how poor we were at consuming the camp rations, plead that we pass them our leftovers. How could we? Why were they so terribly hungry? We soon found out. A few weeks of this diet convinced us how rationed the nourishment really was. It was possible to go on living for some time expending all of our meager energies in a state engulfed by a war effort that required every hand it could get, but this rationing of food spelled inevitable ruin. We also discovered that cases of cannibalism were not unknown in Nazi camps.

After some time, I came to know the sensations of hunger and the reaction of a hungry man to satiety, well. During the roll call, odors of satiety came as if from nowhere, and we had to brace ourselves so we did not faint. The parable of Lazarus is about the hungry, but addressed to the well-fed, it is a parable that is always timely.

"The sons of death!" *(Ps. 79:11)*. Heaps of human bodies were thrown into a pile like dried shavings onto woodpiles; the garbage heaps of camp degradation. That was how it was meant to be; that was the camp program. "Arbeit macht frei!" was written on the gates, and in the governor's speeches we would hear: "Your way out is through the chimneys." The crematoriums were located near the blocks, and their chimneys smoked often. Later, near the end, they could not keep up.

The camps were a death harvest of hunger, cold, heat, inhuman work regimes, and epidemics. The camp rationalization of cruelty was extraordinary. In Auschwitz, it reached its heights, but it was the rule in all of the camps. Each camp was full of its own inhuman triumphs, whether they were in the calculation of food portions, the scheduling of the gas chambers, or the execution of browbeating, torture, and murder procedures. The SS could not keep up, so they employed fellow prisoners, creating new castes of "prominents."

Our first block-chief was a prisoner with a green triangle attached to his uniform, indicating that he was a *Berufsverbrecher* ("professional criminal"). He was not at all the worst of them. Later, our bosses were political prisoners, just like us. In general, with only a few exceptions, they were awful and they were everywhere: in each block room; in the whole camp; in the infirmary; in the kitchen; in the work teams. The prominents occupied the positions of block-chiefs, secretaries, translators, *Lageraltesters* ("camp prefects"), nurses, doctors, crematorium workers, and *Arbeitskommando Kapos* ("work-team chiefs"). They became the camp aristocracy and enjoyed unlimited powers including condemning numbers to death, and even executing sentences themselves. Cruelty and sadism reaped their harvest.

The enormous contours of terror unleashed by the deadly aggression of 1939 opened all doors and encompassed everything.

Why did the prominents do what they did?

Let me pass over the details to ask the question: for what price? These were men of camp privilege set against a background of misery, hunger, cold, and fear. They were men who were well-dressed and well-fed, with food and also with power. These were the heights of a consumerist society based on the abasement of human dignity.

And to think that it was all in the twentieth century!

In the heart of Europe!

Where, in our age, had the old continent gone? And what took place before the world's gaze? Was the world blind, deaf, or powerless? Is it not powerless still—faced with the ascendance of a consumerist culture unmindful of the poverty and misery of so many?

This was how a crazy man, acclaimed as leader, was building the foundations of the Thousand Year Reich.

It is said that in the face of defeat, the *Führer* ("leader") shouted that his nation was unworthy of him. It is well that he still had enough time to spiritually isolate himself from his nation. Hopefully he was isolated not only from his own nation, but from every other nation, as well.

It has been said that the camps demonstrated what man could do to man. This merits elaboration, and would be better expressed, "what a man can do to nations," or, "what a man who claimed to be superhuman did to our nation." Poland is the nation that was represented by the largest number of prisoners, second only to that nation which was, foremost, condemned to annihilation: the Jewish people.

7

Attack on Polish Culture

The Sachsenhausen-Oranienburg camp was located near Kraków, where, at that time in the 1940s, despite Kraków's rich treasury of centuries of learning, barbarity had set in. The Sachsenhausen-Oranienburg camp became the scene of a powerful blow measured out against Polish culture. It was an attack that had the contours of a symbol. Kraków, after all, is the home of the first university in Poland, the Jagiellonian University,[11] associated in name and throughout its history with the greatest Polish royal dynasty. This University was precisely the Nazis' target. Some 183 university academicians were invited to a meeting, only to be arrested in a brutal and primitive manner upon their arrival. They were then transported to Sachsenhausen. (Was it only a coincidence that this Kraków attack preceded the arrests carried out at Poland's oldest seminary by just one day?)

When we arrived at the camp, many of the Polish professors had already been liberated, but not all; the younger academic staff was sent on to Dachau. One professor, Father Jan Salamucha, was annexed to our block.

How could their being set free be explained? In the system that ran the Nazi camps such events were unheard of. It is probable that the arrests aroused worldwide public opinion, but the truth of that will probably never be known. Initiatives were undertaken to rescue the professors. Father I. J. Bochenski, O.P.,[12] a lector at the Jagiellonian University residing temporarily in Italy, was one of the organizers of the rescue effort, and he would recall the events many years later in Freiburg, Switzerland: the personal intervention of Mussolini was secured thanks to Count Ciano, who mediated the organization of a meeting with his delegation. His arguments principally revolved around the special contributions of Poland to European culture, and ended up successfully.

How did the attack on Polish culture unfold?

On November 5, 1985, the Szczecin cathedral hosted a memorial marking the fortieth anniversary of the liberation of Nazi concentration camps. The speakers focused on three camps: on Auschwitz, as the camp of the Holy Prisoner, Saint Maximilian; on Dachau, about which the Szczecin archbishop witnessed; and on Sachsenhausen-Oranienburg, which was discussed by the survivor Józef Wolski (from among the 183 then arrested, twenty were living as of this writing).

The paper on Sachsenhausen was entitled: "Attack on Polish Culture." Although the attack failed, it was paid for by great sacrifices on the part of those arrested, and the deaths of a number of them: twenty-two died in Sachsenhausen, and five died a few days after being set free. The casualties included Stanislaw Estreicher, Ignacy Chrzanowski, Michal Siedlecki, Kazimierz Kostanecki, and Jerzy Smolenski, among others. The attack failed not only because the Nazi authorities were forced to liberate the imprisoned professors, but above all, because in the words of Jósef Wolski: "Almost all the liberated prisoners undertook to work in the underground Jagiellonian University in 1942."

The heavily tested luminaries of Polish culture did not surrender their weapons. That continues to be the marvelous legacy that they have left to us from their time under foreign occupation.

Below are a few fragments of the paper delivered by this surviving professor, which I cannot but cite:

We were invited in an underhand manner to a meeting at the university under the pretences of enlightenment as to the German policy regarding education. We came to experience the German strategy in the realms of learning and internationally approved human rights, however, on our own skins. We recall to this day the resounding words of the German *Sturmbannführer* ("an army rank specific to the Wermacht"), Bruno Muller, who announced that we had reopened the university without consultation (which was untrue), and that the Jagiellonian University was always an enemy of Germany. His words expressed typical German arrogance: reluctance to acknowledge anyone else in the world but themselves. . . .

Still vivid before my eyes is the scene when armored Gestapo officers entered room number fifty-six, and swearing and beating us, began to push us out of the *Collegium Novum* ("New College")[13] into trucks parked on a side street. This is how the long persecution of the university, starting with the Montelupich prison, then the Wroclaw prison, through to the concentration camps of Sachsenhausen and Dachau, began. I remember how, in Sachsenhausen, two young Gestapo officers who harassed prisoners at every opportunity, ordered us to get under the tables and lift them with our heads. The debasement and thoughtless degradation of one human being by another, acquired the silhouette of a symbol here.

But the contrary, the contradiction of this humiliation, was also to be seen.

Professor Stanislaw Pigon cites the last words of his renowned colleague, Professor Estreicher:

Friends, do not allow our deaths to go to waste! . . . Such deaths, examples of steadfastness and magnanimity, radiant and strengthening, are testimonies capable of rescuing and upholding our faith in humanity which is being put to such a terrible test. This is one priceless treasure that can be carried out from the jaws of furious evil. Such was our personal 'catharsis' that commands us to remember the times of affliction and degradation with rightful pride.[14]

Memoirs, testimonies, and historical documents are more than just words on paper; they are also a warning. The task at hand in this respect never becomes untimely, wherever we are. Each new generation has to continue writing our history and living our Polish culture in accord with the words of Pope John Paul II: "Polish culture has Christian roots," remembering also that without culture, man cannot be whole, nor can a nation. No nation can boast a national life divorced from culture.

The plenipotentiary of the West German Embassy in Warsaw, Count Dietrich von Brühl (later ambassador in Vienna), and his wife were also present at the celebrations marking the fortieth anniversary of the end of the camps. Their presence was a beautiful and eloquent sign.

One other very eminent fact stands out: the relics of Saint Otto (bishop of Bamburg and an apostle of Western Pomerania) translated recently to the cathedral, lie reposed in the main altar. This German bishop (1060–1139) had successfully and evangelically converted Pomerania. His mission was in response to an invitation from the Polish ruler, Boleslaw Krzywousty.

It is also worth mentioning that the letter of invitation sent by King Boleslaw has survived through to this day. Its contents are impressive, and evidence a high degree of culture.

Those were the 1920s of the twelfth century. . . .

Polish culture suffered irreparable losses as the result of numerous barbaric war initiatives. These included the destruction of countless pillars of culture, and the leveling of Warsaw to the ground, together with all its great treasures. Losses also came from theft. The occupying forces knew well that the little town of Wloclawek hid a richly endowed seminary library, housing an extraordinary collection of illuminated manuscripts and incunabula. Accordingly, the library was promptly removed to Poznan (from where, after the war, it was reclaimed by Professor Father Stefan Wyszynski and his collaborators). Poznan had been envisaged by the occupiers as a center of new culture for the whole of the Warthegau—the German-administered territories.

Beyond that, however, how can the human losses be quantified? How many of the most worthy people died? How many lost their health, including those Kraków professors who were liberated after a short time in camp? It is hard to believe that they were but a minute symbol in relation to the total losses of sons and daughters that our nation experienced.

Nevertheless, despite those losses and defeats, the Great Resistance forged new cultural values and new spiritual strengths.

The question then remains: What happens to a society's culture when it is engaged in the destruction of a thousand-year-old culture of another nation? The issue is a broad one, and it is an issue that is not indifferent to Europe, or to the world at large.

How can the very phenomenon of disregard for the nation under foreign occupation be explained away without evaluation? Does it not contradict one's own culture, thus undermining it further?

It is worth also posing the question: What is the historical backdrop of this phenomenon? Does it arise from cultural ascendance? Or, rather, does it come from military strategy, which has been to push eastward against the Slavic peoples since ages past—at least since the eighth century? Or, are economic factors decisive?

In regard to all of these areas, Polish history has not been short of great achievements. We have already mentioned culture. Let me also mention that the partitioning of Poland was agreed to only a mere one hundred years after Sobieski's victory at Vienna.[15] It is, however, true that we have never been covetous of others—fighting, rather, for "our freedom and yours." We were not always capable of freely developing our skills and our own economic astuteness. When this was possible, though, as it was in the times of the Piast and Jagiellonian dynasties, and also in recent years, as for example (despite our political feebleness) in the inter-war period, our achievements were impressive. The post-war reconstruction, after all of the defeats we had suffered, can also be judged an achievement. The challenge is to arrive at an objective and honest all-around evaluation.

Of course, the danger of subjectivism plagues all of us; the lessons of history must not, therefore, be taken lightly by anybody. The example of the Nazi war came at a very high price. Let it be the last such severe lesson in human history. Let it serve as a warning to future generations that it never need be repeated again.

The encumbrances to national development, many of which date far back into history, came to be compounded during the Nazi period by a new criterion of cultural assessment: that of racism. It is a criterion devoid of anything wise and humane.

In addition, the Nazi discovery of the destructive power of negative demography came to bear. A short comment here will suffice: "Those loaded terms demonstrate that the aim was to devise methods which could come in useful in the biological elimination of whole nations under Nazi occupation."[16] Are we not faced with traces of this grim undertaking still to this day? The premeditated scheme of increasing alcohol consumption to destructive levels, for instance, has certainly left a mark that is still discernible.

Destroying the human person and his humanity is the very peak of anti-culture.

Let me repeat once again: all of this unfolded in the middle of the twentieth century. Who can gauge how deep its roots have gone?

As to how the values of culture can be defended and spread, steadfastly, even in the clutches of the heaviest enslavement, the Kraków professors gave a response worthy of their great heritage.

8

The Troop Changes

At Sachsenhausen, the Kraków professors departed, but their places were filled by priests, predominantly from the Warthegau. The priests were the servants of a Church which brought culture and learning into the country, and to this day, continues to stand guard over these values. They were educated by the Church to be custodians of culture—personal, social, and spiritual culture—expressed in the truth of faith and praise of God.

In Sachsenhausen, having gotten over the initial shock, these men of God began to search for sources of spiritual nourishment. Talks on Christian asceticism were organized under the auspices of the spiritual director of the Gniezno seminary, Father Tadeusz Tadrzynski. In the theological discussions, two priests distinguished themselves by their fluency in Latin: Father Florian, a Camaldolesian monk, and Father Edward Grzymala. Later on I came to be in closer contact with Father Grzymala. To this day, I still remember his lecture that explained how the Arch of Titus can be considered the synthesis of the art of Ancient Rome.

Bishop Kozal was still not with us. I have mentioned the great spiritual character of this man several times, and I shall have to return to that theme yet again to describe his life's heroic epilogue. When he did come to join us, he was handcuffed and already very emaciated, only to be further singled out and persecuted still.

Before attaining to the heroic deeds during which he never failed to be faithful, Bishop Kozal lived a life of peace. Theresa Bojarska, a Polish poet and prose writer, thus recalls him:

This was a man of great simplicity and deep inborn culture. He loved everything that was beautiful.

The ex-custodian of the Bydgoszcz museum, Kazimierz Biernacki, a witness who testified in Bishop Kozal's beatification process, recalls:

There were no exhibitions that Father Michael Kozal would fail to visit. . . . He was deeply interested in new trends in art, though old paintings were his special passion. I was extremely sorry when he had to leave Bydgoszcz, and later, Gniezno. I continued to hope that our contacts should not be severed by his transfer. His Lordship's letters confirmed this. On August 27, merely four days before the eruption of the war, he sent me an anonymous painting of Christ crucified from Wloclawek. He was very keen that this painting should be restored in our workshop. Unfortunately, we never had the time to fulfill his order. Today it seems to me to be significant that he began his mission as bishop in Wloclawek by giving thought to the restoration of a painting which figured Christ dying on the Cross.[17]

Let us first return to the time of trial when we were suffering in Sachsenhausen, as the bishop continued to suffer in Lad.

Among our spiritual and religious experiences, we were also awakened to the need to entrust our survival to God. We came to understand that only He could save us. The idea to consecrate ourselves especially to the care of Saint Joseph, the guardian of the

Church who was entrusted with the mission of saving the life of the Son of God, was born. The same initiative returned at the end of the war, when those who had managed to survive the camp calamities came to face the heightened fury of the governors of an empire soon doomed to fall.

Needless to say, all of these inner experiences of ours came outside the camp program, or rather, ran contrary to it. Camp life had its own rhythms and wicked manners. Right through from the morning alarm to the evening bells enforcing night-time silence, we were made to stand at attention, carry out various types of work, distribute soup cauldrons, demonstrate various physical exercises, and even engage in sport. The fitness exercises were run by Father Pawel Prabucki. He was an ex-German army officer from the First World War, who later became a priest of the diocese of Chelm. He came to be our *Kapo* ("group chief"), and he was one of three brothers-priests in the camp: Alojzy, Boleslaw, and Pawel, all of whom died. Father Pawel was an exceptionally generous spirit; he drew the attention of the SS men onto himself, and he knowingly tolerated their grotesqueries in order to cover us.

"Sport" denoted just another form of calculated prison torture. We were forced to demonstrate prolonged push-ups, and also to roll in various directions while lying down on the ground. A typical punishment was to have to hold up a bucket of water in a squatting position, with arms stretched straight out in front. All of this comprised normal camp routine. Various camp crimes were punished over and above this in penal companies. Certain categories of prisoners were automatically assigned to these. We could observe them from afar: their constant exercises and marches over very difficult terrain, their heavy work, and their particularly harsh treatment. We pitied them. How long would they last?

Some of my colleagues, as I have already mentioned, departed from us quickly. Apparently they were victims of pneumonia.

Indeed, it came to be very cold; although here in Sachsenhausen, everything was ruthless and harsh. Was it an especially cruel camp? No. There was no such thing as an easy camp, but because this one was situated so close to Berlin it was used as an example for others, and therefore, in all probability, was especially severe and strict.

Then there were the chieftains—the prominent prisoners. What did they have to gain from all the brutality they exhibited? Who were they? They wore various triangles on their uniforms, which meant that their crimes were different. These were men as if from another world—probably because all of them, being more experienced prisoners, already bore the psychological scars of past days and years of camp experiences. Poor men!

Little did we anticipate, in the midst of all of this, that we would come to have a chapel prepared for us in the camp. The news stirred everything that was best within us. None of the obstacles set before us could lessen our joy. It was announced that all the clergy would be allowed to make their way to the chapel every morning, and one of us, Father Prabucki, would have the right to offer Holy Mass. We had to fit this in, however, in the time that was allocated to personal hygiene and breakfast, including the carrying of the cauldrons. Breakfast posed the least problem as it consisted of drinking some dark liquid, which was thankfully warm and bore the name of coffee, and a small piece of bread if there was any left (bread was rationed out once daily and often consumed immediately). The other activities were difficult to fit in the time we had left, however, but of course we managed nonetheless.

Thus, while it was still dark we would all make our way in absolute silence to the allocated camp hall. It immediately transformed into a chapel through our eager prayer. The prisoners filled it quickly, in prayer, and then participated in the Most Holy Sacrifice. Many deeply yearned to offer Mass themselves, and hunger for the Eucharist was virtually palpable in the air around us. Both, in the normal way of things, ought to be unattainable. Some priests asked whether it could be possible to concelebrate, something then unknown apart from the ceremony of priestly ordinations. We had difficulty in finding the appropriate necessities for the sacrament. Wine was nowhere to be found, and we were unsure whether the crumbs of camp bread, baked from unknown ingredients, constituted viable matter? Did the fact that the main celebrant harbored the intention of consecrating the matter in his hands bring about consecration and allow the reception of Holy Communion? There were many such questions born of great yearning for that which is most sacred and most dear—such authentic yearning! This alone was witness enough to the deep faith glowing within all of these men.

Questions also arose as to the possibility of hearing confession. Did the priests here enjoy the necessary legal sanction? The canon lawyers did not exhibit much hesitation. They quickly explained that when life is in danger every priest may hear confessions and give absolution, and such danger was the rule of camp life wherever you turned.

At least our Sacrament of Reconciliation was rescued! Praised be God!

We came to experience anew how important it was to pray together, though we continued to sustain private prayer, as well. We came to cogently experience the meaning of community participation in the Eucharistic sacrifice, strength given by common prayer of thanksgiving, and intercourse with the One who is truly present in the Sacrament of the Altar. I, myself, was not yet able to offer Mass. I did not suffer the personal dilemmas faced by the celebrants of the Eucharist (though some priests shared them, as if to receive counsel)—I only participated. That alone meant a great deal.

I remember those mornings of prayer vividly to this day: the uncertainty as to what awaited me in the coming day; the fear that transfixed me when I thought that that day might be no different than the day before; i.e., an extremely difficult day of dragging freshly cut pines in from the forest. Would my strength last me ıe day when it had already been so faltering the day x of us were allocated to one big tree. This would not have been so awful if our strength had not been so sapped by the previous few months. Then, one day, something was transformed in my poor heart. What and how I did not know. Was it the leftovers of fear, or was it some confiding peace . . .? The day passed unusually smoothly, having thus begun in the solitude of chapel prayer and trustful intercession.

I'm not too sure now whether or not this happy day coincided with a Marian feast day. We all remember, however, exactly how her feast days sometimes heralded particularly fierce storms; the enemy would give vent to his anger that the feast day was a day of her glory. Her days would also sometimes bring about extraordinary transformations for the better—as if the chains of evil suddenly tore apart.

Then December arrived: the month when we came to depart from Sachsenhausen-Oranienburg.

Our parting with the camp differed markedly from normal-life farewells: there were no feelings of sorrow or regret. Perhaps, however, we were allowed some hope—maybe things might get better? After all, we had left behind the little cruel guard Schubert. That alone was quite some relief! It turned out, however, that little Schubert actually came with us. Danger, in its different guises, was also still with us; fear, too, under different forms, clung to us all the time. There was only one way to turn: to Our Lady. *"Pod Twoja Obrone. . . ."* ("We fly to your protection. . . .")

We arrived at the next stage of our journey, and again, there was another set of gates. This time, we were taken to the oldest and best known prison camp—the infamous Dachau.

Schubert disappeared en route, and he was by no means the only one. Who was going to take his place? There was no use worrying: "Today has enough troubles of its own." *(Mt. 6:34).*

9

Winter

The journey to Dachau took place by night, and the morning revealed a beautiful, snowy winter day. We were faced with our first winter in camp—after that earlier winter in the Wloclawek prison and in Lad.

The multiplicity of those experiences has left me, but I still have a few memories now. The present moment impresses itself on the past. At that time, I questioned what was ahead, but that question, too, is circumscribed by what we experienced after getting off the train at Dachau. That experience, though apparently meaningless, was nevertheless both bitter and perilous. That was the way our life had come to be. It was winter, and we were surrounded by the beautiful white snow. Us *Häftlings* ("concentration camp inmates") ought to have been happy to see such a sight. However, the trodden snow stuck to our wooden clogs, which made our march from the railway station to the camp harder and harder because it was impossible to stop to get rid of the snow since the guards keep shouting at us to hurry. The simplest solution was to take the clogs off and continue barefoot. I would have eagerly done so, but earlier, in anticipation of the long march, I had tied the clogs to my ankles with leather straps so that they would not fall off. My companions must have been having less trouble, I thought to myself, but I had no time to look around. We were all shouldering our own thoughts and our own weight en route to one of the most notorious camps of Nazi Germany.

The march turned out to be just a foretaste of what this winter, and the other wartime winters to come, had in store for us. The experience, though minor, was somewhat symbolic: the beauty of winter had been turned into an instrument of torment and oppression.

We eventually reached our destination and it was almost a relief. The snow was falling—one of the prettiest of sights. During winter in Dachau, snow fell often and in abundance. One could follow the reflections of the book of Ecclesiastes:

He sprinkles snow like birds alighting,
it comes down like locusts settling.
The eye marvels at the beauty of its whiteness,
and the mind is amazed at its falling. . . .
The Lord himself having made all things,
and having given wisdom to devout men.
(Ec. 43:18-19; 35)

But we were at a prison camp.

Shortly after we arrived, an officer quickly came up with the idea that they should make the clergy do sport. Thus, whenever there were any breathing spaces in the camp routine, especially on Saturdays and Sundays, the clergy was ordered to clear the whole terrain of snow. We loaded trucks with snow and deposited it into pits. We did all of this to the backdrop of hellish screams from prisoner chiefs of various ranks (the SS tended to keep clear)—it was a nightmare. It was a plot devised by someone capable of turning all that is most beautiful in the created world into derelict ugliness.

Toward the end of April after our winter adventures, our superiors from Lad, including Bishop Kozal, were brought to join us. It was cold with high humidity, and it was beginning to snow again. So much for our belief that at least our superiors had been spared out of regard for their seniority—on the contrary, their journey to Dachau was both prolonged and extremely harsh. They had been beaten, maltreated in various prisons, and ultimately handcuffed in Berlin. This was how the capital city of the Third Reich deigned to honor a Polish bishop and his companions. It was painful even to look at these men, whose coats and warm clothes had just been taken away, standing at attention in their camp pajamas, almost barefoot, with their heads uncovered because the storehouses were short of prison caps. How were they going to survive all that awaited them?

In the minds of the camp authorities, too many of them were surviving too long already, so death was evoked in the form of so-called invalid transports—the first of which took place in that beautiful month of May.

But to return again to winter . . .

In the winter, the *Lagerstrasse* ("main camp road") was invariably slippery. That became a menace—especially when it came to carrying the soup cauldrons, because it was all too easy to spill the contents. At midday we received soup, and in the mornings and evenings we were given some nondescript drink; it was very poor, but all the same priceless, just like the remnants of life it supported. The cauldrons were carried by men who were hurried along by officers that had them under constant surveillance. The men quickly carried them through the kitchen and down the stairs. They moved fast and dangerously across the slippery surfaces, clad in their wooden prison clogs.

On the surface of things, this, too, seemed to be but a minor detail. In truth, however, it was yet another nightmare. The lifting itself was extremely difficult. Our energies were spent, and the weight was enormous. The falls were almost unbearable, and even though they happened more often in the winter, they were also inevitable in the summer. Our bishop fell once, laden with a soup cauldron. The response was unrelenting: the block-chief gave him a furious beating, which triggered an acute earache. Such were the Stations of the Cross he suffered; such were the falls of Christ's passion he shared. They had viciously beaten him en route to Dachau, and they continued to beat him in the camp itself. He went lame from all the beatings, and they also always triggered inner ear infections. This was how he eventually died; this was how his sacrifice came to be fulfilled. Auschwitz and Dachau became a sacrificial stake, ignited by love, though for him, it burnt more slowly. "Thy will be done . . ."

Winter, in all its majesty, failed to cover the awful plight of the prisoners. From time to time, the snowy Alps were visible from afar, but there was no one still able to muster it within himself to give any thought to how beautiful they really are; this can only be done by one who is able to look at the world with the eyes of a man, not of a slave.

Then, what seemed to be the worst of all the winters arrived— that of 1942 to 1943. At least it seemed that way until the snows of 1945, which brought with them the greatest number of deaths.

I have previously given testimony to our experiences during that first winter, which commenced on November 11, 1942 in the publication *The Ten Just Men*. However, I felt that it must again be included in this book, which is why I put it here. I ask that its form be received with understanding, incorporating into this account the text as it already stands. Please understand my situation: the testimony, by any means, must not be dropped, but it would have been difficult to rewrite anew. The psychological strain of recalling these past sufferings to mind is beginning to weigh me down, which comes as much of a surprise, even to me.

10

The Experimentation Wards

Autumn of 1942 arrived while I was at the Dachau concentration camp in the wake of one of the worst summers yet. It was a summer of unending, swelteringly hot days. Nevertheless, prisoners continued to be relentlessly hastened on in their work by the Kapos—a work regime which the malnourished, emaciated inmates could hardly sustain any longer. Inmates often fainted, especially around midday and on the parade ground—sometimes no longer even able to respond to the cold water which was poured over them. The mortality rate rose so high, and the haste from sundown to sunset continued so unrelentingly that oftentimes, even the news of the death of someone very close to us, sometimes even living in the same barracks, would not arrive until days later.

Unfortunately, the arrival of this autumn failed to bring any fresh hope along with it. To the contrary, alongside the usual camp torments we began to receive word that experiments had begun to be performed on prisoners. The rumors were mystifying and gave few details, but nonetheless, they spread fear.

Work on the *Kommando Plantag* ("the SS large-scale agricultural enterprise") was always hard, and in the autumn it was compounded by rain that seeped through our prison rags. We shivered in the cold.

The beginning of November saw our group, which was made up solely of clergy except for our Sub-Kapo, a good hearted Pole, harvesting onions. We had to do everything with our bare hands, regardless of the wet, saturated soil.

It was after such a day bent over onion bulbs, November 10, 1942 to be exact, that our return to the barracks turned out to hold yet another dreadful shock for us. We were suddenly summoned and ordered to stand in line in the barracks hall, as it was already dark outside. Ober-Kapo Zimmerman of the camp infirmary began to inspect us all. Reportedly, he was a plumber by trade, but he often acted as a surgeon in the infirmary, and moreover, he was one of the exclusive camp elite. He measured us up one by one, according to criteria known only to himself, and had the numbers of his chosen prisoners written down.

The ages of those upon whom his choice fell varied, but I was the youngest among them. At this point I was still a deacon, even though I had completed seminary. We were forewarned that the next day after the morning assembly, all the noted-down numbers would be called out and would make their way to the infirmary.

Zimmerman then left. Nobody spoke of the incident, but everybody knew that it concerned the rumored experimentation. An awkward silence fell over us. In me, it was literally a deadly one.

In muted and measured words, I shared how I saw my position with my counselor, Father Stefan Biskupski, a seminary professor of mine. He judged it similarly. I asked him to inform my next of kin if I died, and I gave him the greatest camp treasure I had managed to hide until then: some dried-out slices of bread.

The next day began just as we had been warned: the parade ground assembly, the calling-out of numbers, and the march to the infirmary. In the infirmary we went through a whole day of detailed medical examinations. They were probably intended to rule out the prisoners who, for one reason or another, were most unsuited to the experiments. In the end, twenty stayed on.

I remained among that twenty.

Apart from guesses, we knew nothing, and were informed of less. After all, who would bother to keep mere "numbers" informed of what lay ahead for them!

After the tests and examinations were finished, we were all placed in one ward. The ward was comprised of twenty prisoners, fit and healthy by camp criteria, but condemned—to what, nobody knew.

Then the drawing of lots began. Prisoner number 22 829 (me) drew a card with the inscription "18B." It said nothing else, and gave no hint of the full dread that 18B meant. In truth, "18" was just a consecutive number among our group of twenty, but, as I would later learn, B denoted *Biochemisch* ("biochemical"), as opposed to A which denoted *Allopatisch* ("system of medicine").

The group was divided into two such groups of ten. The division was significant because it dictated what type of treatment we were to receive. Group B, my group, was going to be treated with previously untested tablets, which could only hypothetically bring relief. Group A, on the other hand, was going to be treated with Tibatin, a sulfonamide drug that had already been proven to be effective, along with other conventional procedures.

The purpose of these experiments was to investigate the potential therapeutic effects of certain drugs. However, the reports that were later unearthed revealed that the hypothesis not only failed the test, but also that the "therapeutic" methods proved positively detrimental, and the number of deaths (denoted in the reports as "departures") turned out to be unexpectedly high.

After the drawing of lots was over, we were marched out one at a time. I had to wait quite a while, but eventually, I was marched out. A new nurse named Hermann led me on. A moment later, I arrived at the operating theater and was ordered to lie down.

It was the first time in my life that I had ever been on an operating table. The operation was short. A young SS officer painfully injected something into my right thigh—some mammoth injection! The note taken after read: Three ml flegmone (puss), containing streptococci.

"Get up!"

The same nurse, Hermann, accompanied me on the way back, but his behavior had changed: he was being solicitous. Why? I failed to register any special symptoms immediately following the painful injection; however, not long after everything dawned on me, and when we arrived back at the ward none of my words were audible, only groans. The operation we were subjected to was supposed to take effect rapidly, and that is exactly what I experienced. In fact, immediately after I returned to the ward I laid myself down—once and for all for many months to come—on the bed marked specifically for me: 18B.

Soon, all of us on the ward become fully aware of the dreadful position we were in: only a few hours passed before the first victim, a young Czech priest, died. By some fluke, he and a Dutch pastor had gotten into our group even though we were meant to have been comprised only of Polish clergy.

Four nurses (*Pflegers* and their superior, the *Oberpfleger*) looked after us in shifts, both day and night. That first evening my nurse was on duty: a muscular, vigorous young man, together with, above all, the well-meaning Hermann. Others turned out to be good-willed, as well, including those who came to visit us regularly in the guise of laboratory staff. They were all political inmates, marked with the red triangle like us.

Hermann made a round of all of the beds, and administered to each of us our prescribed drug. He then approached me a second time. He had something important to say: "You're the youngest," he said, "and it seems you're not yet a priest. Tell me the truth: do you believe in God, or not? I'm nineteen and I belong to the Party, and the Party has taken away my faith. How do you believe?"

It was hard for me to speak, and with time, it grew more and more difficult. Moreover, the dialogue was in German (I had been learning the language since I was a boy, but it had always been very difficult for me). The next day, an elderly priest from Poznan said to me: "You speak German poorly. Why did you take on such a difficult discourse?" But Herman had approached me, and I was convinced that it was my solemn duty to speak.

At midnight, Hermann's shift ended, and with it, the discourse. The lights went out. Only a small red one remained above the door. It remains vivid to me till this day.

My energy had left me almost entirely. I was persuaded of this when I tried to make my way to the toilet even though it was very nearby (my bed was located right by the door). My pain was not yet such as to force me to groan, but my total weakness gave me much cause for concern. The nurses must have been aware of this, because when it came time to change my station in the morning they carried me with care, much to my surprise. When they sat me down for a second on a straw mat, my weakness proved too much and they had to jump to my help as I fainted.

I often returned in my thoughts to that first exchange with Hermann, though we never resumed the conversation as such. However, in a way it did continue through his friendly compassion, even though it always remained hidden behind the haughty exterior of a German youth walking about the ward in a manner which seemed to denote that he was too tall to see what he saw. He too was the youngest. He had more right than others to question why he was there. Perhaps this was how he reasoned. Perhaps this explained why he gave the impression of being elsewhere. I do not recall whether he ever laughed, but thankfully he was more friendly and compassionate than all of the other Pflegers on duty. He somehow knew when the pain reached such a threshold that it needed controlling. When I asked him whether the painkillers could become at all addictive, he'd just curtly answer: *"Nein!"* ("No!")

The discourse Hermann began proved to be the first in a chain of dialogues that evolved on the experimentation ward. It also anticipated their scope: they ranged from those spurred by well-meaning care for a person who had become the object of experimentation, through to heated debates about God; from encounters without words in an atmosphere of goodness, to silent encounters in a context of inhuman coldness.

This coldness was ingrained in the Commission doctors. Doctors! How could they be doctors? Also heartless was our blockmaster, Zier. I happened to meet him once in the corridor, and I tried to smile as best I could, but in response I received only a cold and merciless stare. Amidst all of this, however, Heini Stöhr, a nurse, and a few others managed to tip the awful scales for the better. Heini was a rather quiet man, but he was careful, caring, and good. Even so, he wasn't the one who gave me the crucial advice I needed, though; rather, I got it from Hermann at the conclusion of our first conversation:

The injection was dangerous. The experiments will be harsh. To survive, one must want to live, and believe it to be possible. Look, over there is a communist whom we are trying to rescue as only we can—and all for nothing. He cannot believe that Hitler ultimately may not win, and so he does not want to live on.

How different his approach was to that of one of my colleagues, who by some fluke, visited us at the ward (before the injection) and said to me: "It's probably just as well that you're here because things are very hard out in the fields!"

My discussions with Franz, another man who worked in my ward, followed. They were not just questions about God, but often heated debates about Him. The experimentation ward was just the beginning of these dialogues. They continued outside the ward on the Lagerstrasse long after. As a rule, they were comprised of methodical and cool debate, open to argument and reason. Franz would constantly come up with new points.

After some time, I began to sense that reasoning was not what really counted. What was the crux of the issue? Perhaps it was precisely the grace of Faith, which had been waylaid somewhere. Was it through his own fault? Did he know this? He spoke enthusiastically of the struggles of the Spanish Civil War, of men who impressed him, and also, in an almost ceremonial manner, of a girl who exceptionally impressed him and who said farewell to him with an honest, chaste embrace. That's how he spoke!

Then, in the beginning of the spring of 1945, I saw Franz walking through a large infirmary hall that was full of survivors, including myself, who had pulled through typhoid (yet another epidemic which claimed the lives of so many who were still alive). He was passing through as a guest, because he had since been made Kapo of an infirmary in one of the subject camps.

At first he failed to recognize me, even when I called out in a muted voice: "Franz!" He came up to my bed, however, and looked though my chart in disbelief. After a while he remarked: "You've survived typhus after what you've already been through! Unbelievable! You Poles have a tough constitution! Yes, and now you'll be saying that it is That One who saved you"—and he pointed ed upwards.

It was hard for me to hear. After all, he was a good and noble man. He and Heini had both worked to rescue us.

I tried to respond. I tried to tell him: "Franz, you always spoke ill of us clergy. Yet you probably know that it was our priests who went to the typhus barracks while yours fled from them; they'll all fall sick and many will die!"

"The good ones will die," he responded. "And the others will come out of it and continue to lead people astray."

His answer pointed out the uselessness of all reasoning, and the futility of words in the face of unsurpassable hard-headedness. This mystery is already depicted in the Gospels, but when standing face-to-face with it, we lose our wits.

I ask those who are reading this: Please pray for my Franz, who was then so young. There is nothing else that can be done.

A small, slim, and totally bald laboratory assistant also made his way to us from time to time. He took blood samples from us every two days. (He was probably the one who warned Heini that I was on the brink of septicemia.) He was an agnostic philosopher. "Man is weird," he would say, "weird even for himself. When my favorite dog died I could not get over it. When, on the other hand, in camp, I received news of the death of my brother who died in a different camp, it almost failed to make an impression."

The exchanges with this laboratory assistant were never long. He had a manner of speaking into the air, as if not wanting a reply. However, since he spoke at all, perhaps he did want something. He was very dexterous in his work, and probably also exact. Regardless, he was for sure friendly.

In general, as I have already mentioned, they were all friendly. When they tried to convince me to choose another way of life, not the priesthood, it was not out of cruelty: rather, they simply failed to understand the priestly vocation; they understood their own family happiness, for which they yearned. When they joked with

Father Czeslaw Sejbuk, editor of *Catholic Mission,* that as a Jesuit he was a member of the Pope's Gestapo, this too did not imply mockery; it was just their sense of humor. Father Sejbuk never responded to these jokes, and in general, spoke almost nothing. He'd only smile sometimes. He had an extremely hard time, and died literally from bed sores.

There was no will or energy for feelings of joy in this dreadful experimentation ward, because we faced frequent operations (Father Kasjan Wolak, a Capuchin monk, Father Baczyk, and Father Suski each went through at least seven) and saw many departures to eternity. However, despite all the horror of our situation, some form of social life did develop. From time to time, though very infrequently, someone would come from the barracks to visit us. More often we would be visited by patients from neighboring wards, or by priests belonging to the next experimentation group (number four). Somehow, they had less of a hard time, so every so often one of the priests would appear, clad in a blanket, to say something, hear something, or just to look.

My conversations with Father Gitschel, a Polish priest of the Society of the Divine Word from Zimmerdienstu, generally did not concern my illness. He simply assisted, when necessary, in a simple and helpful manner. He became my confessor—my intermediary in that exchange between God and myself.

There was one other special dialogue of mercy which I cannot help but recall.

Toward the end of 1942 we were granted permission to receive food parcels. Such permission in a camp of death by hunger was utterly unbelievable. The first snippets of this news filtered through camp quite rapidly, but quite a while went by before the first real parcel reached one of us. Father Leopold Bilko, who occupied the bed right next to mine, was the first to get one right at the end of December. Father Gitschel unpacked it for him, and Father Bilko somehow mustered enough energy to divide out the contents. He never asked any questions of all the hungry mouths that emerged from the corners of the infirmary, lured by the long-forgotten smell of normal, real bread. He asked no questions; he just divided out portions that signified much more than just slices of bread or pieces of ham. Rather, the food represented joy and hope; it was as if he was giving out pieces of his own heart. At the end of the distribution he turned to me and said: "There is really almost nothing left for us." Then after a moment of thought, he continued, "But you see, we had a spiritual father in the seminary who would advise us that if we felt reluctant to part with anything, we should do so all the more hastily, without delay."

It was not just me that Heini managed to save. After the liberation it turned out that he also saved Father Bilko. A Samaritan rescued a Samaritan.

Odd things, even great things, would sometimes happen on the ward.

Heini, as I have already mentioned, was generally quiet, but in reality, he was a man of real dialogue. His dialogue was not of words alone, but one of a heart full of solicitude. His skills were not medical, but he somehow managed to tip the scales initially set by the cold indifference of the inhuman doctors. Aloof and unconcerned—that was how the doctors entered this ward of acute suffering. Sometimes they rattled on about their own day-to-day affairs. They exhibited no feelings whatsoever for these "numbers," for these guinea-pig men, as they saw us. Heini, however, compensated richly for their behavior by his compassionate care for the individual. This caring attitude, as later transpired, was capable of taking on the greatest of risks.

Although Heini displayed no outward sentimentality, he nevertheless exhibited an almost motherly sensitivity through his eyes, his short, stuttered remarks, and his authentic disgust with the persistent state of sepsis we were undergoing. He was a sensitive man, both in his care for all of us sick men he tried to help, and in his efforts to elicit exemplary nursing care from the other personnel. He was always direct and always delicate (a true nurse, even though in real life he was a craftsman). He willingly asked questions, never made bitter remarks about religion (which were generally unrelenting in camp life), and never trumpeted his own convictions. He was said to have been a socialist.

That compassionate Heini—his image stands vivid in my eyes to this day.

The dialogue of continuous care later evoked a short exchange of words at a decisive moment of life or death. It was precisely this exchange that fully bore out the price Heini was prepared to pay for his humane attitude toward the individual.

But for the present, I must return to the chronological account. It will provide a clearer background to that exchange and to other dialogues, as well.

The period of initial experimentation, which lasted five months in all, ought first to be recorded in greater detail. But how? Each day is a history in itself.

The beginnings reverberated with fear. The High Commission, headed by *Sturmbannführer* ("Storm Unit Leader") Dr. Schütz, was quick to instill this in us. The committee was comprised chiefly of SS men, but there were also some civilians, one of whom was reportedly a Berlin professor. They came to our ward every day. Schütz would dictate, and Father Steinkelderer, an Austrian prisoner, had to take down exact notes. I remember that the High Commission once deigned to stop a bit longer at my bed— number 18B. After having diagnosed a critical inflammatory state, evident across the whole of my right thigh, the commission issued a decision not to perform incisions, but just to wait and observe how my condition would evolve over the next eight days.

Thus they waited, and I, the object of their investigations, lived on. After the eight days, a first incision was then attempted. After I came out of the anesthesia, I found my whole leg on a rail, bandaged in swathes of tissue paper. During the first change of my dressing (initially dressings were changed under water) I was able to see the drains which had been inserted. It struck me what it meant to drain human muscles: the dressing changes were atrocious. Even the SS men would turn their eyes away. It hurt. Acute pain would engulf me even when somebody passing by my bed caused the floorboards to tremble . . .

I was warned that if even one drop of septic puss entered my bloodstream I would die. However, this did not concern me as much as it normally would have, because it was not possible for me to make even the slightest movement.

The state of high inflammation in my leg persisted, so I underwent two further incisions. I have no idea who the SS men who carried them out were. Perhaps they were practicing surgeons—perhaps not. I do, however, know that the third incision was carried out by a real surgeon, a Pole named Dr. Czarkowski. By then, the death rate in the camp had reached such levels that real doctors were actually permitted to work at the infirmary, which was a big concession.

Heini was there. He would wake us up. I can't be sure today whether it was always him, but I remember how he woke me after the most painful operation I underwent: smiling, optimistic, and trying to say something friendly despite the fact that, as a rule, he smiled and spoke little.

Meanwhile, other members of the third experimentation group were suffering and dying next to me. (We had just learned that we belonged to group three. Group one was comprised of Jews who all died, and group two was made up of professional criminals, among whom two ultimately survived.) After my nearest neighbor in the ward, Father Józef Kocot (a philosophy professor from the Oblates' Seminary), died, beset by vicious *Schüttelfrost* ("piercing frost"), I found myself next to Monsignor Leopold Bilko. Our beds were adjacent to one another, and there was a tin under his pillow that contained the Most Blessed Sacrament. That meant daily spiritual nourishment in the form of tiny particles of the Eucharist, after regular Confession.

There was one priest on this terrible experimentation ward who circulated among the beds—the dear Father Gitschel. He was one of the *Zimmerdienstu* ("the equivalent to a hospital auxiliary"), and accomplished even the least pleasant tasks his work entailed quietly and with dedication. He endured these tasks in order to be able to perform those higher tasks of hearing Confession and administering the Body of Christ.

I remember one particularly hushed Sunday, when the Dutch pastor, Tundermann, died. We tried to do something. His case was reported to the doctor on duty, an SS officer, who came and ordered the body to be uncovered. Tundermann's trolley bed was right next to my own, so I saw his body clearly: it was entirely yellow, like wax. Heini suggested administering a dose of Tibatin: "Perhaps we can still save him?" The SS man then asked, "Which group does he belong to?" When someone told him he belonged to Group B, the SS man responded with the verdict: "Leave him to die!"

It was nonsensical, but the criminal experimentation had to be taken to its end. Things had to be precise and accurate, and the protocols had to be followed to the letter—that one precept had priority over all other considerations.

Nevertheless, something spoiled the timetable. It became clear that "my thoughts are not your thoughts, my ways not your ways—it is Yahweh who speaks." *(Is. 55:8).*

One thing that visibly rippled the schedules was the High Commission's fear of epidemic: one's own life becomes very precious when other people are being coldly murdered. An epidemic of typhoid fever had just erupted in the camp; the commission, therefore, adjourned its meetings.

This news, alongside that of the retreat from Stalingrad, heralded the New Year of 1943.

I felt neither better nor worse for it. I had been effectively immobilized by the experimentation which had begun on November 11. I felt no despair because there was God. There was always need for prayer, but never more so than prior to the incision procedures. Each one was like a final departure. It was only prior to the third and last one, the most dangerous one, that I was able to reach out to Father Steinkelderer, the High Commission's Austrian secretary. He discreetly gave me Extreme Unction (the former name for the Sacrament of the Sick) as I was laid on the trolley.

Among my meditations I also eagerly implored Our Blessed Mother to save me. I promised her that if she rescued me I would somehow find a way to make a pilgrimage to her shrine at Jasna Góra. That was my dream, and my faith sustained it. So things were not so bad, and I was relieved that the High Commission had stopped coming.

A few days into the New Year, Heini came to see me, clearly very anxious about my condition. He literally cursed my persistent inflammation. He departed, only to return a few moments later with Franz. After a short consultation, they transferred me onto a trolley and relocated me to a nearby ward run by a young Czechoslovakian, Zdenek Zamecnik, who was clearly someone that Heini trusted.

We had a short conversation—one that later turned out to be crucial.

My interlocutor was Heini, the others only listened in. "You are in a poor state," he began. "You are in danger of septicemia. I hope to rescue you, but you must keep total silence about this, because if this is discovered I'll lose my head and you too will be killed."

"I give my word I shall keep my silence," I replied. "But tell me, do I have any chance? It is important for me to know."

"We're trying. Tibatin has proved to work in many such cases. We'll start injecting you. In a second you'll receive the first shot."

The exchange came to an end, and the needle was inserted. Total silence prevailed. Exchanges which decide between life and death are often brief.

The injections were repeated many times. The whole ward was amazed when my never-ceasing dressing changes were no longer necessary. Finally, they took off the rail. It was unbelievable!

In total, my stay on the ward still lasted a long time, but there was peace. Peace thanks to the epidemic.

Thankfully, inspectors no longer came. Their visits were dreadful because they were always associated with the threat that one or another might find himself on the so-called "invalid list," which meant the gas chamber. It was very logical. Who would risk allowing witnesses of such immense crimes to continue living?

But despite everything, those who survived, survived. "My thoughts, not yours . . ."

In 1975 these survivors gave testimony at court in Munich. As a Polish bishop, I told the full truth, but in the presence of witnesses, much to their astonishment, I forgave Dr. Schütz (who had become a renowned doctor in Essen-Bredeney). Why were they astounded? Could I not forgive him?

Then, many years after those incidents there was another testimony (which itself is unbelievable—how is it I could live on so long?) This one was about Heini Stöhr—how different it was from the one of Dr. Schütz! Who is man? What are his capacities? How inconceivable is the range of their characters? At one end you have Dr. Schütz; at the other Heini Stöhr!

I very much wanted to meet up with Heini after the liberation. I never managed to do so, but I can send Christ's words to his address in eternity: "Whatsoever you do to the least of these brothers of mine, you do unto me." *(Mt. 25:40).*

As for Schütz? Forgive me that I still mention him. I do so not for contrast's sake, but by way of seeking out a difficult truth about a man. Dr. Schütz did not want to let go of my right hand when I concluded my testimony in court: "But we can look each other in the eyes," he whispered. "I had to do it. But I did less than I had to. . . ."

Does the criminal not belong among the poorest of creatures on this earth? Only God's never-ending mercy can judge.

Pope John Paul II's 1980 encyclical, *Dives in Misericordia* ("Rich in Mercy"), explains such truth for our difficult times; times taken up by civilization's gigantic struggles between good and evil.

"Whatsoever you do to the least of my brothers . . ." Schütz humbly renounced his own past. Heini earned the place of a just man. The full Gospel verse ought to be cited here:

And then the just shall ask: "Lord . . . when did we see you sick or in prison and come to you?" And the Lord shall reply: "In truth I tell you: Whatsoever you did to the least of my brothers, you did unto me." *(Mt. 25: 37, 39–40).*

It bears mentioning that it is indeed a great grace ever to be, in life, one of the "least of his brethren."

After surviving and leaving the ward, I learned that Bishop Kozal did all he could to rescue the only Wloclawek seminarian who had been allocated to the experiments—me. It was all for naught, though. Maybe this was meant as one more drop in his cup of suffering. The cup was beginning to overflow, however. Winter saw the bishop pass away from us, but his departure only served to heighten his aura of sanctity. The news, which shot through the whole camp on January 26, even reaching the experimentation ward, made an unusually deep impression. Despite its own horrors, the ward had to suffer even more by the sacrifice of its spiritual father.

Even in its final stages, his departure resembled an Auschwitz type of death: his illness lasted too long, so things were sped up with a lethal injection.

The similarity goes much deeper yet: that same Spirit that had led others in Auschwitz, also led Bishop Kozal along the way of Love, right through to the ultimate sacrifice.

The sacrifice of so many Polish priests bridged the distance between Auschwitz and Dachau. It also bridged the distance in time between the twentieth century and the early martyrs, the first followers of the apostles. We read about one of these in the Book of Revelation:

Write to the Angel of the Church in Smyrna: "This is the Alpha and the Omega, who was dead and has come to life again: I know the trials you have had and how poor you are, though you are rich. Do not be afraid of the sufferings that are coming to you. I tell you, the devil is going to send some of you into prison, to test you. . . . Even if you have to die, keep faithful, and I will give you the crown of life for your prize." *(Rev. 2:8–10).*

These holy words refer both to Bishop Polycarp, that Angel in Smyrna, and to Bishop Michael, who was marked out by Providence as an Angel to that chosen part of the Church suffering severe oppression in the Dachau concentration camp. He, too, went through oppression and abjection, but was nevertheless blessed with much and faithful unto death when thrown into jail to be subjected to trial by the Devil. Both he and his brethren, as it was with Saint Polycarp, proved worthy of the wreath of eternal life, which the Lord himself, the Alpha and the Omega, bestows.

The Lord's witnesses. Faithful ones. "Faithful unto death!"

11

Yet Another Epidemic

The winter of 1942 to 1943 was marked by a typhoid fever epidemic, as I have already mentioned. Then, the next and last winter, the winter of 1944 to 1945, was stamped by a dreadful epidemic of typhus.

How did it come about? Sauberkeit—the regime of shining floors and leveled beds—clearly did not ward it off. Rather, it was used as yet another instrument of oppression; something to wrack our nerves before the high inspections. The call, *"Hoher Beuch kommt!"* ("The High Commission is approaching!"), was always a cry of alarm for us. As to personal hygiene among the prisoners, Sauberkeit was of little use. The camp never ceased to be a breeding ground for vermin and germs. Under such conditions, a typhus epidemic could not help but erupt.

How did the disease first reach the camp? On several occasions, since I was an experienced häftling, I remember being forced to help register the *Zugangs* ("newcomers"). All of them had special cards among their paperwork. Some of these cards bore the inscription: "typhus." Why, then, were they transported in such a state to another camp—to Dachau?

The *Dolmetscher* ("camp translator") was a distinguished man named Richard Knosala. He was a genuine man and a genuine Pole from Olsztyn. Before the war, he had been a teacher of German in his home town. He strived hard to help at least some of the Poles who were brought to join us after the downfall of the Warsaw Uprising, and also some of the Hungarians who belonged to Miklos Kallay's government. That government had betrayed the Führer, and so its members were all dispatched to camps, including Dachau.

I personally bore a special respect for Istvan Szent-Miklosy, the long-standing Undersecretary of State in the Hungarian Ministry of Foreign Affairs. He told interesting tales of caution. Among these were descriptions of visits he made alongside the Prime Minister to the *Führerhauptquartier* ("Führer's headquarters"). Much was whispered abroad about these headquarters, but nobody knew where they were located. I asked him about this and received the reply: *"Bei Allenstein"* ("Near Olsztyn"). Astounded that he revealed this aloud, I informed our head "politician," Father Joseph Bialy. He, too, was surprised. Undersecretary of State Szent-Miklosy had both sense and foresight. Did he ever expect to return home to his family? He died shortly thereafter—a victim of the epidemic.

And now back to the translator, Knosala. As it turned out, he was able to fulfill his hopes of helping us. The times proved more amenable as the young SS "wolves" were, at last, dispatched off to the front lines. Older replacements came along, but they were not as good at carrying their SS uniform with that so-called "dignity." They also made no secret of being hungry and malnourished themselves. Hunger set in once again as the war effort put a stop to any post- and private-supply lines. However, discipline was lessened so people's own shrewdness could devise ways of obtaining some means of survival. Supplies were really very scant, but they meant much to us. Some items reached camp thanks to "organization." That word, in camp jargon, usually denoted theft, or rather, the reclaiming of the bare necessities for life from the ones who had earlier stripped us of them. It became possible to share things with the older reservists from the SS forces. Among them, however, was some of the "old corps" who tried to make sure that everything stayed the same as before. They remained blind to the approaching end of the Thousand Year Reich. Most of them, nonetheless, did not have to wait long before meeting their own terrible ends.

Knosala was on particularly good terms with the head of the camp post office. Together, they decided to establish a post office *Arbeitskommando* ("work team") in order to set up a new archives system. The work was fictitious (nobody needed any new files); the intention was to save the lives of a dozen or so prisoners.

The workplace of this new Arbeitskommando was a dream considering general camp conditions. We were under a roof, seated down, and in heated rooms—nothing could be more ideal! I was put in charge of the group. The task was not a simple one, and when we passed through the gates they always sought evidence that our Arbeitskommando had been approved by the central authorities. We never managed to get such central approval, but somehow, we always got through the barriers. On one occasion, we even met Camp Commander Weiss at the gates. His policy then was to spare those who were still alive since he always needed more labor. The number of workers was beginning to get too slim. Each passage through the gates turned out safely, though it did not spare our nerves. Strip searches were always a possibility; they took place often, and in a brutal manner. The SS always managed to find something, too—for example, pieces of newspaper stuck to our freezing backs, or some half-rotten "stolen" potato.

Is it possible to get rid of acquired phobias and fears? I do not know. I also do not know why it is that to this day, I hate border crossings, even when they are swift and civilized. Is there no way to spare ex-camp inmates the ordeal? They would certainly appreciate it.

The most blood-curdling incident our Arbeitskommando group experienced, however, took place away from the camp gates. One day, Knosala came to our workplace and anxiously whispered to me that typhus had taken hold of the camp. Who would have expected that precisely this relatively strong and remarkably fit prisoner could turn out to be one of the first victims of the epidemic? He departed from us shortly afterwards. Thus, we suddenly lost our friend who had managed to turn the meager powers allotted to him into the benefit of so many others in the camp. Knosala gave witness as to how the human spirit could be preserved under conditions where it could just as easily have been enslaved. He never renounced his freedom, and he remained "faithful until death."

Meanwhile, things that were previously unheard of began to happen in the camp. Corpses were being carried out in heaps from the barracks that were hit hardest by the epidemic. When all of the prominents ran away from these barracks, the Polish clergy moved in to assist the sick. That was what the Lord commanded: "Whatsoever you do to the least of my brethren. . . ."

The epidemic did not spare our own barracks (now block number twenty-eight because number thirty had been made into a sick ward). People kept telling me to be extra careful, because after going through the experiments, my heart would not be up to coping with such a disease.

Nevertheless, I caught it; although the symptoms, apart from the sheer exhaustion, were not clearly discernible. It was decided that I should go to the infirmary, where I could take advantage of the acquaintances I had made earlier (people still remembered the experiments vividly). I was taken there without going through the compulsory parade ground ordeal where the SS officers would usually decide who should be admitted to the hospital.

I asked my rector, Father Korszynski, to hear my confession. He came to me, moved by my request. The confession then took place with me lying on a bunk bed.

Two colleagues of mine then carried me, wrapped in a blanket, out of the barracks. That was how the dead were usually taken out, so apparently people made signs of the cross over me from afar. I needed them, even though I never saw those gestures of friendship. By then, I saw nothing.

I was admitted into the infirmary without trouble: a big success! However, problems later ensued. I was taken to the bath house where the next contingent of sick inmates was to arrive shortly, via the official route from the parade ground. I recall being laid down on the concrete under the shower heads, all ready for the routine bath, and having to wait there. Thankfully, the concrete was not cold because the baths were heated, and my body temperature was also high.

I did not expect to be put in this position, but it did not worry me too much. The waiting dragged on. I had once seen a baby bird that had fallen out of its nest onto a country lane. The picture came back to me: I was that little bird. Then I took up a measured self-defense reaction—one that also was dictated by some remote memories. Water began to drip from above and I began to rub my temples. This was symbolic of my will to live on. Perhaps it was an expression of hope. I had not lost hope even for a moment.

Did I pray? There was no other option!

Finally the other sick inmates were brought in. Cascades of hot water were poured over us, but only for a few short seconds. A good nurse then lifted me up and put a shirt on me right away because there were no towels. He also wrapped me in my blanket and handed me some clogs. Then we moved off. The way was not long, we were just going to one of the neighboring barracks, but en route there was frost and snow.

When we arrived at our destination, everything was silent around us. The nurses were calm and almost courteous. "Stand up straight!" But I could not. "Well then lean on something. We must examine and weigh you." They handed me a thermometer, weighed me, took my pulse, and finally, wrote down some notes and set up a chart for me. I looked at it and recalled something I had heard somewhere before: if pulse and temperature intersect, things are not well. Mine had just intersected.

Suddenly, the sirens began to bellow an air-raid alarm. This had begun to recur often lately. We were in total darkness. The nurse led me out into a large but silent space, and sought out the place designated for me. Once he found it, he helped me get up onto the upper bunk, where I was allotted the space at the very edge.

It began to get cold. There was hardly any straw left in my mat, although some still remained in my pillow. I tried to maneuver it under my back, and I straightened my arms out alongside my body. I thought that perhaps that way I might manage to ward off the frost. Through the silence I heard wheezing and groaning. The room was indeed very large. It contained a crowd of people, but it was silent.

What was going on?

I did not dare to think about it much. I fell asleep, and by the time I woke up it was already daytime. In the daylight everything was both audible and visible, but the silence still resounded in my ears. The area was filled to the brim with patients—on bunk beds in my row, and down below on single beds which I could observe from above. Their immobility was as if everything on earth had suddenly halted. But within me, there was peace.

A nurse in white uniform slowly paced the hall. What could he do to help? Someone was with me, though, clad in an even whiter garment. Yes, I understood! It was Mary, my mother! She was in the midst of the great abjection being suffered by her children. She could not leave us! She was here! In truth, she was nearby, and she was in white . . .

Who was lying beside me? He did not look European, with his dense beard. He was clearly unconscious. Could anybody hold a conversation here? No. There was no chance and no will. I, too, did not have it in me.

The inner peace continued throughout this encounter with the mystery of death. Was it that the silence signified death, or was it death that was so silent? Anyhow, it was silence that prevailed, not hopelessness.

Below me, I recognized a fellow Pole—our barracks secretary. The nurse went up to him to change his shirt; somebody probably sent him over. The nurse helped him into a sitting position in order to take off his old one. At this juncture, something almost invisible happened: all came to a halt. The thin dividing line between life and death was crossed in the blink of an eye, and almost in utter silence.

The silence continued and the hours passed by. How many? Nobody could tell. Why should they?

Two SS doctors came along. They said nothing. In the usual course of events a ward round would be announced and they would circulate and inspect everything. This did not happen, though, so we thought that they must be up to something. However, they were not shouting. When they entered, no one exclaimed: "Achtung!" and no one stood to attention (which always happened in the infirmary, including in the experimentation ward). The officers seemed to be harboring some sort of good will within themselves. In any case, when they ordered me to get down and try to walk I did not feel any dread. On the contrary, it almost amused me. Why? Perhaps it was my own awkwardness, or perhaps it was because there was someone in uniform looking upon me without anger in the concentration camp context. The very encounter with some sort of human good will disarmed me.

I was then transferred to a different barracks where I was again examined: are there any patches or not? I fell unconscious. They transferred me once again; how many times, I have no idea. When I awoke, I again found myself on the top bunk. It was lighter, but still crowded. The dear Father Steinkelderer brought me Holy Communion, but how was I to receive it? My throat was as dry as a parchment. He helped me, and I managed to get a few drops of the nondescript liquid down.

Then another unexpected incident came—one owing to somebody's great care. Friends smuggled a little container of boiled fruit through to me. How did they manage it? What a treasure! I held it, as if falling asleep and dreaming about it. I did fall asleep. Then, just after I woke up, I reached out for the jar. What a disappointment! It turned out to be empty! After quite some time went by, a German I had gotten to know told me that he had seen the foreigner next to me drink all of it after he noticed that I had passed out. "I thought he did the right thing," my friend continued. "You are not fit for life anyway."

The next typhus ward that I was sent to was once again in a very large hall. The beds were only in single tiers, and the sick were already naked under their blankets to make it easier to carry them out to be cremated when they died. It was a waiting room where the illness was left unimpeded in deciding its own course— either choosing life or death. There was one lone man that circulated among the beds: our helpless guard. A Lagerstrasse was shaved onto his head, so he must have been a Russian. (There had been an earlier time when this was applied to all of us, but by then it was restricted only to citizens of the Soviet Union.) I talked to him, and he turned out to be a doctor. I entrusted him with my little box of medicines. My friends, again, had managed to smuggle it through to me. He looked through it, taking his time, and administered what he saw fit. He hardly spoke a word, and I wondered what he was thinking.

I was then transferred to my last typhus ward: the convalescent barracks. (It was here that I met Franz, as described in the previous chapter on the experimentation ward.) I was laid next to a Spaniard who had an unbelievably accelerated pulse rate. He seemed unlikely to pull through. My heartbeat also began to race like mad. So, when Dr. Fijalkowski, the barrack attendant, informed me that I was to return to my block I reacted with surprise: "But Doctor, my heart goes mad with the slightest exertion!" He tried to calm me down: "You will continue to have heart trouble for the next thirty years or so."

During this time, I was visited by Father Henry Korczala. After preparing me gently, he broke the news of the death of my close friend Jurek Musiol, a Jesuit novice. Then, another one of our mutual friends described to me how he bid farewell to him with the words: "Jurek, see you in eternity!" By then Jurek no longer heard anything—or maybe he heard all the better!

Many died—very many. Among them, a Dutchman surnamed Van Ruys, who had been brought to Dachau for his participation in the *Nacht und Nebel* ("Night and Fog") campaign, helping the Allied parachutists. An excellent portrait painter, he invited me to come and rest in his French Riviera resort after the liberation. He, too, left for another "resort" before this could come to be.

The crematorium could not keep up. The Allies filmed the enormous heaps of the departed when they arrived. It was an unearthly nightmare.

Nobody who was found on the heaps will ever stand up to tell his own story. Let this testimony of mine serve as theirs as well.

The Dachau winters were times of indescribable torment, given the infernal camp routine. At the same time, those winters were times of heroic suffering and self-sacrificing deeds of service by people who did not flinch from putting their own lives on the line. Heroism came in different shapes and took various courses. It is impossible to describe all such deeds and all such heroes—but that is not of the utmost importance. After all, their names are written down in Heaven. *(cf. Lk. 10:20)*. Their deeds are recorded also, for "a man can have no greater love than to lay down his life for his friends." *(Jn. 15:13)*. The Church cites these words with reference to the first saintly concentration camp prisoner to be canonized, Saint Maximilian Kolbe.

These just men—how many are they in number? May they shine like stars in the firmament of our Heavens. And let them bend down over this earth, which is after all, the work of the God of Love. . . . Let them intercede, praying that his creation cease to be subject to such dreadful destruction at the hands of men possessed by hatred.

I will refrain from walking in the footsteps of that great author Nobel Laureate Wladyslaw Reymont,[18] who followed the seasons of the year in depicting Polish village life. Let his hero Boryna's love for his land be reborn and endure, as is essential for the survival of these royal Piast people.

Having made this reservation, I will nevertheless have to give some picture of Dachau in the summer. Meanwhile, let us take somewhat of a break, as Dachau summers turn out to be scarcely more bearable than the winters.

12

My Power is Made Perfect in Weakness

In both Sachsenhausen and Dachau we were allowed access to a chapel, which came as a surprise. However, we were also surprised when later, after a brief period of leniency, access by the Polish clergy was barred. Even in this area, we were differentiated from clergy of other nationalities, and discriminated against. Different treatment was meted out to us; much harsher demands were made of us.

The figures speak for themselves: Dachau held clergy from twenty different countries, but the number of priests from Poland far exceeded all of the others combined.

This was borne out especially in the inhuman overcrowding to which we were subjected, as opposed to the conditions in block twenty-six which housed all the clergy from the other countries. They had enough room within their three halls to house everybody in comparative comfort. The fourth hall served as the chapel. Blocks twenty-eight and thirty, allocated to polish clergy (as well as Protestant pastors), were by contrast forever crowded—and more and more so as new contingents arrived from other camps to replace the deceased. The conditions became even more extreme, however, when block thirty was taken away. After all, Dachau was a concentration camp, progressively "concentrating" its prisoner population, including the Polish clergy, into tighter and tighter quarters. Army chaplains were also brought to Dachau from the prisoner-of-war camps, though this was in contravention of the Geneva Convention.

Let me cite Father Wiktor Jacewicz, a historian, at this juncture:

The Catholic Church in Poland experienced great human losses during the Second World War. Before September 1, 1939, the number of diocesan priests throughout Poland stood at 10,017. From among these, some 20 percent met their death in prisons, executions, and concentration camps. 30 percent were persecuted by the occupying forces. In all, the war years eliminated some 50 percent from active pastoral service. In addition, the losses experienced by religious orders, both male and female, must be taken into account. The situation was all the more tragic considering that, in general, the clergy who were fit and active, the ones most capable of outreach and missionary work, suffered most. The Golgotha where Polish clergy underwent the greatest repression was the Dachau concentration camp.[19]

The entrance to the chapel was always ardently guarded, but we refused to let resignation prevail. We attempted to visit it regularly, both individually and in groups. The security was tightened, but we kept renewing our efforts.

The SS also kept watch. It seemed, however, that the officers made their way to the services out of personal curiosity. Without removing their hats, they would constantly look around without the slightest reverence for the Holy of Holies.

Thanks to the chapel and the daily offering of the Holy Mass, Communion was shared out among us every morning.

The first time I was able to participate in the Holy Encounter in Dachau was on my first Christmas Eve spent there. My friend, a Jesuit seminarian, asked me out of the blue whether I would like to receive the Lord Jesus. What a surprise! After that, the Lord's Table became a daily experience. The so-called "catacombs" of the *Schlafraum* ("sleeping quarters") allowed this, as warnings were able to reach us there while the enemy was still in the *Wohnraum* ("entrance hall").

With time, under the veil of total secrecy, Holy Mass began to be offered in our own block, as well. An intensive Eucharistic life became, once again, as it had been in Sachsenhausen, the source of all our spiritual strength as we confronted the camp torments. We, his priests, now suffered with Christ, and for Him.

In regard to candidates for the priesthood, the situation was *pari passu* ("moving at an equal pace without preference"). By then, we were quite numerous, especially including those of us from religious orders. The grace of the Eucharist also reached out to several of our lay brothers whenever possible. Unfortunately, however, the occasions were few. Holy Communion was also given out among our work teams—needless to say, under the veil of utter secrecy.

In the evenings, when the discipline was slightly more lenient, once everybody had reached their place in the Schlafraum and the light was switched off, Father Joseph Bialy, a Poznan parish priest, would usually deliver a kind of political commentary. He would share what he had read between the lines in the available newspapers, especially the main Third Reich daily newspaper, the *Völkischer Beobachter.* Next we would pray, and then there would be a short meditation. I remember most of all the reflections on the Advent antiphons which Father Alexander Wozny preached. Sometimes sporadic, sometimes more regular, we maintained spiritual links with block twenty-six.

Father Joseph Kentenich, the founder of the Schönstatt Movement[20], sometimes visited us. It was there, in Dachau, that he collaborated with a layman, Dr. Kühr, to set up the so-called *Familienwerk* ("Family Work"), which is still an integral part of the movement. We were also sometimes visited by the renowned Belgian, Father Leon de Coninck, and by Carl Leisner, who came in his capacity as a priest only on one occasion (in former years he had visited us as a seminarian). Leisner came to give us his first priestly blessing with the little energy he had left, after saying the only Mass he ever would offer, on December 26, 1944.

Leisner was ordained a priest in camp (the only such case in any concentration camp). He contracted tuberculosis after his arrest, and by 1944, his energy levels had significantly dropped off. Bishop Gabriel Piguet (1857–1952) of Clérmont-Ferrand in France was a fellow inmate, and after secretly obtaining the necessary approvals, ordained Leisner, who by then, was on his last legs. Following his ordination, Father Leisner offered his first and last Mass, on the feast of Saint Stephen. That was why his spiritual confidante, the Jesuit Father Piess, later entitled his biography of Leisner: *Stephanus Heute* ("Stephen Today").

Although I participated in these extraordinary events, I never again had the chance to see Leisner—the friend I made on my first day in camp. At present, intense efforts are underway to promote the beatification of Father Leisner, particularly on the part of the International Carl Leisner Circle, which, among other places, is active in Poland.

The beatification process of Father Kentenich is also underway.

We had reasons to be grateful that God gave us so many gifts as we yearned for his love. We found them in the obtaining of the chapel, in the unceasing hunger for the Word of God and the Eucharist, in group and individual prayer (for example, in that prayer with Father Stefan Biskupski out on the fields), and in scripture sharing. The Sacrament of Reconciliation was available, in secrecy but in serenity, usually in free time in our block. At the clandestine Holy Masses we had the Holy Presence. Even when the chapel was unavailable, they could not hinder the One "Who is." *(Ex. 3:14).* "He is" present in the sacrament and present in His promise: "Where two or three are gathered . . ." *(cf. Mt. 18:20)*; He is present in the carrying of our cross, my cross, first carried by Himself. "I shall not leave you orphans," *(Jn. 14:18),* He said, revealing the mystery of the Holy Trinity and His own oneness with the Father, and promising the coming of the Paraclete. We were baptized according to His will. As to the hosts of the un-baptized who were so awfully persecuted, shall they not be enveloped by the Grace of God by some ardent desire for baptism?

When asked how he coped with the parade ground ordeals, Father Grzymala would reply: "I adore God, One in the Holy Trinity." He also believed Trinity Sunday to be the greatest feast in the liturgical calendar.

The younger ones in our group came up with the idea of a Holy Confraternity—a spiritual community for those who wanted to belong to it. Its backbone was formed by a group of Jesuit seminarians under Kazimierz Chudy and Julian Plachecki. Father Vincent Frelichowski became its animator. Father Boleslaw Burian helped him, and later, after the liberation, became the spiritual father to the Polish Seminary in Paris. The Holy Confraternity was based on two precepts: first, to live every present moment in the love of God, as perfectly as possible in all we experienced and did; and second, to join on the spiritual level at nine o'clock every evening, together with the whole community, in a spiritual antiphon to Our Lady.

How deeply I am struck later, during my return to my fatherland, by the realization that here, too, at nine o'clock every evening people stand and pray an antiphon to Our Lady of Jasna Góra.

A figure of Our Lady stood in the Dachau Chapel, in Block twenty-six. We had no access to it. But how can you keep a Mother away from her children—her very abject children?

Amid this Way of the Cross that was the camp, Christ's words: "Whosoever wants to follow me . . ." *(Lk. 9:23)*, came to life. How many saints there were amidst the suffering! The camp was a place where Jesus just kept repeating: "Today you shall be with me in paradise." *(Lk. 23:43)*. How else could it be seen?

I am reluctant to start a litany of names. No one knows all of them well. Once again, Jesus' words about the names written down in heaven come to mind. *(cf. Lk. 10:20)*. Every survivor can enumerate many names as evidence of the identity of Christ's witnesses, and the survivors can be asked about them as long as time still allows. For many who could have given testimony, time has already ended. Soon, nobody will be left.

The fear of starting off a litany of names arises because no one person can produce an exhaustive list. No one person can give testimony of all, even with the utmost dedication to the cause. So, perhaps I will give at least some examples—not many, just the more conspicuous ones. Let me try, even if it be in a small way . . .

Bishop Michael Kozal: he followed his way of martyrdom with such serenity and dignity, even though it was a way of such extraordinary suffering. He was "faithful unto death," like Saint Polycarp, the bishop-martyr of Smyrna.

Monsignor Henry Koczorowski: one of my dearest spiritual fathers and our rector. He was always incredibly hard-working and systematic, always a disciplined ascetic, and in camp, radiant with serenity and cheerfulness. He was taken on a transport of invalids to the gas chambers, together with so many other priests. (Just for being priests!) At the last moment, he saw a friend of his brutally hit in the face by a wild *Stubenaltester* ("a person in charge of cleaning a block"), just for trying to say goodbye to him.

From among all the priests:

Father Dominic Jedrzejewski: a parish priest from Goslawice near Konin, I remember his steady, bright, calm, and unlined eyes, and the serene power of his, "No," when camp authorities proposed to let him go free (after extraordinary efforts on someone's part) if he would renounce all priestly functions. I also recall that he shared a friendship with the young seminarian Tadeusz Dulny— one so full of charm and mutual support.

Father Grzymala: a walking encyclopedia, but above all, a priest of great faith, constantly contemplating and deeply adoring the Holy Trinity, One God. He was known as a remarkable preacher. When, on one occasion, his preaching of the Word cost him a vicious beating, he rejoiced that thus he could "have the honor of suffering humiliation for the sake of the Name of Jesus." *(Acts 5:41).* At the end, utterly emaciated, he was taken to the infirmary to be designated immediately for invalid transport.

Father Joseph Staszewski: a parish priest at Saint Stanislav's parish in Wloclawek, he was straightforward, and almost naïve, but dedicated to God without reservation. He was also an excellent confessor.

Father Czeslaw Domachowski: a parish priest from Samarzewo, to whom I would so much wish to apologize for an overly critical remark I once made as a seminarian. (It is easy to judge at that age!) Dying, he gave this beautiful testimony: "Please tell my parishioners that I offered my life for them."

Father Theodore Korcz: an exemplary priest, he was hardworking, conscientious, and a good organizer; he accomplished a great deal for of all of us, acting as our block-master during the last stage of camp life.

Father Joseph Szymak: a parish priest at Rozinów near Wloclawek, he was a renowned preacher and man of charity. He appeared to be strict, but he had an extraordinarily sensitive heart.

He was broken by the news that the parish church built by him with such difficulty was dismantled on order of the occupying forces. (We later learned that the dismantling of churches was commonplace.)

Father Vincent Frelichowski: a vicar from Torun, he was such a generous apostle to the poorest in the camp. He died a heroic death, from his dedication to the sick dying of typhoid. His beatification process is underway.

Father Leon de Coninck: a Belgian Jesuit and a pastoral theologian from Louvain, he was one of our closest foreign friends. He was an excellent speaker, especially in regard to the human soul. We eagerly listened in to him in the chapel whenever we could get close, and also when he came to visit us. He was a man of wise and serene disposition, and close to the struggles of others.

Father Joseph Kentenich: founder of the widespread Schönstatt Movement, he was ardently devoted to Our Lady. By force of this, he was close to us in heart. An ascetic, thinker, and lecturer, he would also visit our Polish barracks from time to time.

Father Michael Riquet: a Jesuit, his gifts as a preacher, later to be borne out in Notre Dame Cathedral, first became apparent in the camp.

Father Carl Leisner: a seminarian ordained to the priesthood in the camp just before his imminent death—he had contracted tuberculosis before his arrest. I met him on my first day in the camp. Since he was the only one among the German clergy who had not yet been ordained, he was quite isolated, though very independent, disciplined, and prayerful. He could always be found near the altar in the Sachsenhausen camp chapel. He seemed to be an incarnation of Saint Paul's words: "Put up with your share of difficulties, like a good soldier of Christ Jesus." *(2 Tim. 2:3)*.

From among the seminarians:

Bronislaw Kostowski: a man who remained faithful and dedicated to his vocation, even to the point of offering up his life.

Stanislaw Grzesitowski: a friend from my class who likewise, as the reports say, could have avoided the invalid transport if only he had renounced the priesthood.

Tadeusz Dulny: extremely obliging and very cheerful. I watched as he died. During one lunch break in that awful summer of 1942, we could see him beginning to faint. Malnourishment and emaciation were taking their toll. Somebody handed him a slice of bread, but it was too late; he hardly managed to bring it up to his lips.

Jurek Musiol: a Jesuit novice and an excellent organizer, both resourceful and obliging. Strongly dedicated to his vocation, he departed from the camp along with the host of others who had contracted typhoid fever.

Among the laity:

Richard Knosala and Istvan Szent-Miklosy: both radiated outstanding virtues of spirit. The two, one a Pole, the other a Hungarian, were bound by a spontaneous camp friendship.

Juliusz Tarnowski: a historical figure, but nevertheless, a man of great simplicity, wisdom, and ardent patriotism. He was from Sucha in the Podhale district.

Edmund Michelet: an outstanding Frenchman, he was another layman whom we would often see among clergy. He was the informal leader of all the Frenchmen in the camp. A personal friend of General Charles de Gaulle, he later become a representative to the United Nations and a leading politician in post-war France. As a statesman and a family man, he was an exemplary Christian, and is a candidate for the honors of the altars.

The Kuder brothers: they were examples of living faith and Christian courage. Faced with death, they saw it as a passage to true Life.

The names of very many others—and these only in Dachau—are written down in heaven.

It is clearly important to correctly understand the situation of the priest inmates.

Many had to depart from this world through the gas chambers solely because they were priests. Many, for this reason alone, had to endure appalling outbreaks of hatred in multiple forms, so heinous that no chronicles can do them justice. Even quietly whispered prayers awakened brutal response! The fury instigated by the Rosary, and the screams, "Stamp on it!" whenever one was found, were unbelievable. It could only have been a satanic rage when one Capuchin seminarian was forced to speak the altar-server's responses while hanging from a pole (a terrible punishment whereby one hung from his wrists, which were twisted back). The same satanic fury was always watching out for the slightest indication that some häftling might be a priest.

But this was the way things were. Such sufferings opened up the treasury of graces won by God's saints: we were dead wheat grains which fell onto the ground "to yield a rich harvest." *(cf. Jn. 12:24).* In truth: "However great the number of sins committed, grace was even greater." *(Rm. 20).*

Did human weakness come to bear on us? Of course it did. Camp life stripped us naked and rendered us unmercifully transparent. However, human weakness alone is not a person's downfall: "My power becomes perfect in weakness." *(2 Cor. 12:9).* His downfall comes when he fails to recognize his weakness and obstinately persists in it.

The hunger alone debilitated and humiliated us: capturing our imaginations; stealing into all our thoughts and discussions. Our memories faded. It is impossible to adequately describe an unrelenting hunger that drags on for years and years. One has to experience it to understand. By no means is hunger a physiological phenomenon alone. Hunger encompasses one's psychology, conquers one's imagination, and claims its rights savagely. I never saw cannibalism in the camp, but there are witnesses of it. Hunting for potato peels was normal. I once saw a group of young people throwing themselves at a trolley of carrots, oblivious to the fact that it could result in their being killed on the spot.

In the midst of such physical trauma, was there still any space for internal advancement in love? If such existed, it came of saintly determination.

I bow my head as I recall examples of priestly faithfulness to God, and of love and ardent concern for our country, which shone through the bleakness of the infernal regimen. Intellectual aspirations of the prisoners should be seen in the same light, all the more so as they were often entirely eclipsed by the "burdens of the day." *(cf. Mt. 20:12)*. However, as soon as these burdens were in the slightest way alleviated, they immediately came back to life.

The priest barracks were an oasis of intellectual endeavor amid the barrenness of the camp at large. Wherever possible, study was included in our daily routines. This was coordinated from above to assist our group of seminarians along our way toward the priesthood. We also studied in private. Foreign languages caught on with enthusiasm. Edmund Michelet became our French teacher. Unfortunately, it turned out that he was unable to include me in his study group, explaining to me as a friend that he could not take on any more students, having accepted responsibility (informal, of course) for all the French prisoners. Nevertheless, he found another teacher for me: a medical student from Toulon named Senes. He was intelligent, literate and . . . did not know a word in any other language but French—much recommended for one who wants to learn a language. When we ended up in Paris later, my effort to learn French (incomprehensible to many at the time) paid off immediately.

From time to time, we managed to get our hands on some sensible books. That's how, at one point, I got a book in German from the Schönstatt Center called *Organic Ascetics*. It made a big impression on me, and I pore over it thoroughly.

The atmosphere that pervaded the group into which I was placed as a seminarian was an atmosphere that was decidedly ordered to spiritual and intellectual values.

Finally, there came a moment that awakened the enthusiasm of all the Polish prisoners. Toward the end of our imprisonment, extraordinary things began to happen: not only were football matches held, but Polish artistic productions were staged. They impressed everybody, and they happened to be directed by Polish clergy.

How right Saint Thomas Aquinas was in his conclusion: *Genus humanum arte et ratione vivit!* ("Humankind lives by art and reason!")

The governor of Dachau, Martin Gottfried Weiss, began to allow "humanity" back into camp life. Even if his intention was only to bolster the physical strength necessary for us to work, its consequences were benevolent: it helped the survivors last out until the liberation.

But we were still a long way from liberation day.

The grace of martyrdom is a unique privilege. The Lord God takes His time preparing men for it. In that context, we can perhaps better understand the camp. The mystery of this greatest of struggles is: "to conquer evil . . . with good."

Did everybody conquer the evil? Nobody has the right to judge men thrown into such infernal circumstances. We leave that to God, the ultimate judge. Meanwhile, we sing the *Te Deum,* the hymn of thanksgiving, for each one who did conquer with good—there were hosts of such men.

Cardinal John Wright, late prefect of the Congregation for the

Clergy in the Vatican, once wrote in a letter to his brother Cardinal Stefan Wyszynski:

> The conclusions drawn by Dorothy Thomson, a journalist without political or religious affiliations, about the witness given by the priest prisoners, are telling. In interviewing survivors from Dachau, be they Jews, men of learning, or political persona, whatever their class or nationality, she would ask the same single question: 'In the midst of the hell which life at Dachau boiled down to—dehumanizing, degrading, and humiliating men—who were those who managed to keep up their dignity and their senses the longest? Who were the men who were capable of forgetting their own abjection to assist others through their suffering in this hellish regime? Who kept their own identity, their dignity, their hopes . . . when around about others lost their lives and faith?' The answers which came were always the same: 'They were the Catholic priests!' They knew why they were there! They knew that all that remained was to give witness! Their dedication, their vocation . . . ! They knew everybody was waiting for their witness: their fellow inmates, their brutal oppressors, and God Himself! They knew that their calling was to give witness, whatever the conditions, in imitating the Only Man, the Only Vocation, Jesus Christ, the Eternal and Greatest Priest, the Faithful Witness to God!"[21]

13

Summertime

Neither autumn (as at Sachsenhausen or on the experimenta-tion ward) nor spring (even despite that Holy Week when the whole community of Polish clergy was condemned for a so-called crime committed by one of us) could ever bring out the dread of camp life as acutely as the wartime winters and summers.

Our first summer in camp was in 1941, and it was much the norm; that is to say the details of camp life as I have previously described suffice to give a picture of its monotony. I say monoto-ny, but it was a monotony where fear lurked behind every corner and at every step, and death stared frequently into our eyes. In camp, death basically had this privilege at any time.

The fear—I was not alone in suffering the fear. It frequently encompassed all of us as a group. I was often able to observe the desolation it sowed, and how it paralyzed its victims the way a boa constrictor hunts its prey. Is it true that fear is hypnotic? It is enough that it terrifies you.

That was how one such drama that unfolded in front of me came to an end. For quite some time, the barracks were being pre-pared to receive large contingents of Russians, but they never arrived. What happened to them? The question remains unanswered. Then a small contingent—somewhere over a hundred—did arrive. It was rumored that their political activities were being investigated. Perhaps that was why they were still alive.

I was assigned to some work inside the camp precinct, and from there I could see the parade ground. On that sunny afternoon, the SS officers marched this new contingent through the empty camp (everyone was at work) up to the *Jourhaus* ("the main gate"). It soon became obvious that the new arrivals were to be executed immediately. The SS officers, armed of course, were relatively few in number. They led out the condemned in small groups. Gunfire resounded in the vicinity of the crematorium. . . .

Eventually, all of them were led out in turn. On earlier occasions I had seen how the Russians were able to exhibit wild courage (there were many comrades in the camp), but these men were utterly tame. Was theirs a courageous approach to death? Maybe; however, I couldn't help but think that I was witnessing the paralyzing effect of fear overriding any capacity to react to the prospect of death. And what a death it was: not one in battle or in any struggle; rather, it was one that was faced with the full anticipation of its inevitability.

The parade ground at Dachau was relatively large. However, it seemed to shrink when each block was marched out to its assigned position—a maneuver not easy to coordinate. The march resulted in faultless rows of ten each, accomplished while singing aloud. The orders, *"Ein Lied!"* ("A Song!") and *"Laut!"* ("Louder!") often reverberated throughout the march.

The rows were always faultlessly even, and the singing was always loud. Where were we able to get the stamina to achieve this? After all, we were on our way back from long hours of work in the scorching sun, with almost no food in our bodies. Someone often had to be carried, but that often heralded the last few seconds of that someone's life. How much misery—due to human mean-ness and human deception—was hidden behind those showpiece marches and loud songs! In some camps, an orchestra played to accompany the inmates returning from life-threatening stone quar-ries. (But also think how many they left behind each day!) During the singing, the music, the gymnastic exercises, and the standing to attention, we had to look at the slogans "Sauberkeit" and "Arbeit" that were written on the rooftops—words in yet another antihu-man and deceptive guise.

The correct interpretation—the conclusion I reached shortly after crossing the camp's threshold—was that this was Satan's king-dom. Can one stay silent about this? Is it legitimate to think that what once was is never going to return? Is it possible to hope to build a more humane world if we run away from the truth of the past?

Every day the routine was repeated: the parade ground was suddenly peopled with a crowd of several thousand standing frozen in silence. The *Raportführer* ("camp inspector") received reports from each of the block masters, and checked them by personally counting the inmates. When he did this we had to stand straight at attention in our disciplined rows . . . anticipating. On occasion, something did not add up or someone would be missing. Rare attempts at escape (how and where to?) still occurred. At these times, the whole camp had to stand waiting on the parade ground, and be collectively punished for the escapee. This continued until they captured the culprit and brought him to the square to punish him. With everybody watching, they would stretch him out on a bench and beat him to death for "education's" sake.

Camp life as a whole was a punishment. For what? From time to time the punishments became extreme in their devices. Their most frequent cause was the so-called reports. Everyone who had the slightest power was able to report an inmate rather than punish him on the spot if he believed that such spontaneous punishment, such as beating him in the face, was too lenient in relation to the "transgression." The most frequent forms of punishment were the pole, from which the prisoner would hang by his twisted wrists for no less than one hour, or the scourging with sticks by the SS with the inmate stretched out on a type of saw-horse. The usual number of strokes allotted was twenty-five, with the prisoner having to count them aloud himself. If he happened to make a mistake, the whole ordeal started over. Other punishments included the so-called penal companies, and then there was the prison block. . . .

On the other hand, there was also an *Ehrenbunker* ("cell for the privileged") for prominent prisoners, to which we had no access at all. Father Johannes Neuhäusler, a German, was one such prisoner who stayed in the Ehrenbunker. He was later named auxiliary bishop of the Munich archdiocese, and he also authored several books about the camp. It was he who founded the Carmelite Monastery of the Most Precious Blood at a location directly neighboring the ex-camp, aligned to the main camp road. At present, a chapel dedicated to the Mortal Agony of Christ, built in 1960 at the instigation of Bishop Neuhäusler, stands at the opposite end of this road. In 1972, we hung a commemorative plaque there, having concluded from our first common pilgrimage of priests and bishops to Dachau in 1970 that there was no noticeable commemoration of all the Polish inmates of the camp. This is not a case of holding anything against other nationalities; it is only that we should speak historical truth about ourselves without relying on anybody else. Knowing that all historians must base their accounts on documentary evidence, we must not neglect that either.

Let us return, once again, to the parade ground.

How can comparisons be drawn between seasons, given that the whole camp must assemble on the square three times a day regardless of what time of year it was?

The winter climate became menacingly dangerous when we were forced to stand motionless, outside, in scant clothing. Some tried to cover their backs with pieces of paper (there were plenty of newspapers about the camp for propaganda purposes), but this carried the threat of being reported. Many tried to keep surreptitiously moving, though the parade ground, in essence, meant standing motionless. On some occasions, we were forced to stand for hours on end on our block street. This was slightly easier because it entailed group exercise, and sometimes we were allowed to huddle into a bunch. On the parade ground, though, such possibilities were precluded. Winter torments on the parade ground were worst for the sick. They had to await the SS verdict—would they be sent to the infirmary or not? A brief glance was followed by a final verdict, often worded: *"Ab!"* ("Get out!")

However, the full dread of the parade ground ordeal became most apparent in summertime. By the summer of 1942, the utter emaciation of the prisoners who were in Dachau for any length of time, including those who arrived in December of 1940, was apparent.

In camp, the day always began with "lights on," and ended after dusk with "lights out," regardless of the season. What resilience the prisoners had to muster to face up to the demands of such long days! We were constantly working; constantly under the vigilant eyes of guards; constantly subject to screaming orders like: *"Bewegung!"* ("Get a move on!") and *"Los! Los!"* ("Quick! Quick!")

It was also imperative to remember to write, on the camp paper and to the approved address, at least the following to our next of kin: *Ich bin gesund und fühle mich wohl* ("My health is good and I feel well"). Who could conceive how difficult this would be? We were so short of both time and energy.

Time, measured by the slow burning-out of a prisoner's life force, seemed to drag out never-endingly. Quietly, amid routine work, someone would ask the question: "What time is it?" Much patience and much effort were needed to last until the shout: *"Werkzeug sauber machen!"* ("Clean your tools!") and the signal: *"Antreten!"* ("Assemble!")

I was assigned to work in the fields. I accompanied Monsignor Stanislaw Bross, a man much older than I was, but who could walk normally, whereas I could only drag my legs along. I was embarrassed, but as time went on, my energies became even more spent. I recall how I once looked over to my neighbor, Father Joseph Gawora from the Katowice diocese, and it appeared, for all purposes, that his end had arrived. By then we could tell. The next day, indeed, he did not turn up at work. We were told he had suddenly been released.

Later, after liberation, he spoke of his miraculous deliverance, and did so as long as he lived. He burned himself out in priestly zeal in thanks to God.

I also remember talking briefly to Father Florian Niedzwiadek, a Camaldonesian monk. He looked odd, dressed in an old frock coat. (That was how we were dressed by then, so as not to waste the clothing left behind by the dead.) There was no time for cracking jokes, though. He complained of feeling faint. It was as if his end had arrived. . . .

We worked in the crop fields; thankfully, they were not stone quarries. There were plenty of herbs around, and even flowers. But even so, it was still the infernal camp regime.

During our short break at noon we had to march back to the camp precinct to receive our hunger rations, wash and polish our bowls, and *"Antreten—schnell!"* ("Assemble quickly!")

It was during such an Antreten that Tadeusz Dulny one day failed to hear, but he had to make it to the parade ground at all costs nonetheless. Everyone did. The dead and the half-dead had to be carried. The latter could no longer stand, so we would lay them down. The obliging (political!) prominents would pour water over them. Sometimes this helped, but sometimes nothing could help any longer.

The numbers waiting to be admitted to the infirmary were always high, and hunger alone reaped a dreadful harvest of mortalities. The prisoners lost weight until they began to look like walking skeletons. Then edema, ulcers, and abscesses (one of the results of the pseudo-medical experimentations) would begin to take over. All these prisoners yearned for the infirmary, which was believed to denote at least some peace and quiet and a length of bed somewhere. It was seen as the last hope. Only later did it become apparent how misplaced this hope was.

Fatigue alone, if complained about on the block, came to be considered an easy excuse for placing a prisoner on the invalid list (which brought about a new criminal device—the gas chamber). The block chiefs drew up the lists, and they had plenty of opportunities to do so. The lists afforded an easy way for the block leaders to eliminate anybody who happened to be *aufallen* ("displeasing"), be it only in appearance.

If that was the situation on the blocks, how much worse would it be in the infirmary? The invalid transport idea reaped its greatest harvest there.

For sick priests the criteria were even more lenient: all would get marked out for transport regardless. Many departed that way, and even if they regained their energy before the transport was organized, it was to no avail. There was no way to cross anybody off the death lists.

The lists often included invalids who had no idea of what awaited them (the invalid list secret was not deciphered until quite late). The individual person was stripped of all his rights, including the one right that civilized people never deny even to criminals: that of being made aware that one is to die.

Auschwitz immediately comes to mind, along with its horrendous statistics: 4 million victims from so many nations. How did they all die? It was there that the most awesome and terrible records were compiled. But one thing was true of all the concentration camps: death fought vigorously for victory over life. Such was the first law of camp life. The inevitable course of events whenever man tries to take power over life and death away from God is no different: the barriers give way, the brakes cease to work, and there is no stopping the tide.

It strikes me how this power, removed from God, is generally exercised with exceptional efficiency: sometimes with sadist appetite, sometimes with indifference, but always with efficiency. That is why they made us stand in file in the baths and march past an SS committee. Merely by waving his hand, one of the committee members indicated which way we were to go: right or left, death or life. As prisoners we were still unaware that this was their way of issuing death sentences. When we were spared, it was only for the time being, though, because in the long run we were all meant to die.

Is it possible to get used to death? Is it possible to become indifferent? One answer is severe: if you didn't you could not survive. Yet the human heart must remain a human heart, even when witness to mountains of dead bodies; even when coming across the dead unexpectedly, for example, in a washroom corner. The human heart must, however, brace itself; it must prepare itself without becoming indifferent.

The camp was a place of death: no euphemisms can be of any help here.

Is it, then, possible to become accustomed to death?

Forgive me for repeating the question. Forgive me, for it is more than a rhetorical question. It is more than a historical one. It is a present-day question. Who taught the trade of killing at that time? Who is still teaching it today? No excuses can help here. "I am the Lord, your God. . . . You shall not kill." *(cf. Ex. 20:1, 13)*. Then and now, the question is one of death, the fruit of killing.

It used to be thought that the Second World War would begin where the First ended. This was not far from wrong. During the first, the efforts were limited; however, during the second they were extended to encompass millions, not only on battlegrounds, but also in camps. Progress and discovery: the "blossoming" of the twentieth century! The rule of technology is unabashed and comprehensive, even up to the point of taking over the area of human life and death. Can it happen when someone wishes it that way? Or, perhaps not just when one, but many, wish it to be so?

It is the age of technology. Good. Let technology be of service to man; let it be of assistance; let it even take over some of his tasks. However, never let it become lord and master over us! Technology must never be allowed to take away our humanity in any area—especially not in that fundamental realm of life and death. Neither life nor death should ever be abandoned to the rule of technology, nor should they be stripped of their fully human character. Mankind must not acclaim this power that belongs only to the Creator.

Life or death is not only a wartime question; it also concerns times of peace—especially in this age of technology. In fact, above all, the question concerns peace. How many people are still being killed? How many people are currently collaborating in inhuman interference into the secret realms of life's beginnings? These technologies are clearly becoming more and more refined, but what about man? Is man developing?

Man, when allied to technology, turns out to be capable of allying himself against life. But, it is he, himself, who remains responsible, not technology as dictator. Man always remains man. Let man always remain man in the knowledge that humanity is beyond price.

14

In the Service of Evil

amp life encompassed everyone: victims who were dying and the oppressors who were carrying out the killing. Who were these killers? They were people after all. How did they stop being human? Sadism cannot explain everything.

"Conquer evil . . . with good." What are the many servants of evil like?

There were so many victims and so many oppressors. What happened to their humanity when they became oppressors? What happened when they stopped their work of persecution? All along they were people, inhabitants of the same planet as we.

Bonum est diffusivum sui ("good radiates and is contagious"), but evil, too, spreads like a disease.

The contingents that arrived at Dachau from France toward the end of the war were a dreadful sight. The freight trains that carried them from the land-camps included compartments where no one made it alive. That was the plan. They were given nothing to drink the entire time, even though it was in the heat of the summer. Moreover, the floors of the wagons were covered with chalk made out of quicklime and chloride, so that whenever anyone would urinate, a cloud of acidic steam would burn and peel their skin. We felt great pity for the few who actually survived, but were then still led to the bath-house, hardly able to stand up. Did we pity them? Me and some others did, yes, but not everyone. I observed with dread the cruelty that fellow inmates were capable of. Their reasoning: "We've been suffering here so long, and you've just arrived! . . ." The human heart can harbor such evil spirits when it becomes infected with the venom of abiding hatred.

Such was the bleak backdrop to the heroic spirit of all those who conquered evil with good.

As long as a human being is still alive, he has the chance to change: "God takes pleasure not in the sinner's death, but in the turning back of a wicked man when he changes his ways, to win life." *(cf. Ez. 33:11)*. During camp life, we were subjected to communal punishment, our tormentors systematically invoking the concept of communal accountability. But how can the man who denies his own accountability convert? How can someone who blindly believes that his highest authority lies in *Befehl* ("orders"), that is, in acting according to orders, ever change his ways? *Befehl ist Befehl!* ("Orders are orders!")

The matter is an important one. It is important to be on the lookout for it, and to warn one another of it in all societies. It is even more important in those scourged by dictatorship, whatever form it may take. The human person must never turn away from his own accountability, blaming everything on others—this will only lead to a dead end.

After the war it was often necessary to ask the question: "If 'they' are to blame, who precisely are 'they'?" Was it only one man and his closest entourage? What, then, is the responsibility shouldered by all those who would scream at the top of their lungs and with enthusiasm: *"Sieg heil!"* ("Hail (to) victory!")

Human responsibility and accountability should never be

underestimated or taken lightly. It is no joking matter. It is an irreplaceable human trait, and as human beings, we never have the right to disown our human traits.

We also must never underrate the dangers that lurk in our weaknesses. "The man who thinks he is safe must be careful that he does not fall." *(1 Cor. 10:12).* Thus goes the advice of an experienced and inspired man, Saint Paul, who himself was often unjustly imprisoned.

It happened once that a group of the more cruel SS officers admitted to Father Prabucki that they had once been Catholics. Were they boasting, or was it nostalgia? Whatever it meant, it was an experience to be noted—a cautionary one. Faith is a great value. It is responsible for a person's formation, for his Christianity. Christ's words come to mind: "Well done, you good and faithful servant! . . . Come and join in your master's happiness." *(Mt. 25:21).*

Life in a concentration camp was a drama—a drama of faith—played out on the level of life and death.

It was compromised, however, by a dreadful faithlessness: the infidelity of people who had radically turned themselves against humanity, which necessarily implied that they had also turned against God, yielding desolation.

15

Dreams of Freedom

The last winter in camp, the one marked by the typhoid fever epidemic, saw the war front move very near to us: the Allied bombing of Munich became both frequent and dangerous—history having turned a page since the 1939 raids. The saga of war was drawing to an end. What that meant for us was anything but clear. Common opinion did not allow for the possibility that we might be freed from camp. How could this be reconciled with an order of things driven by hatred?

After we were finally liberated, we discovered a transcript of an order that precluded our being delivered to the Allies alive. At the time, I doubted the authenticity of the order. It was worded according to the circumstances under which it must have been delivered to the camp authorities. However, one thing later convinced me that the document was true to the original: the explanation included the reasoning that when the prisoners were liberated from Buchenwald, they treated the civilian population cruelly—yet another typical propaganda claim, widespread since the war first began.

One way or another, the serious dangers that threatened the

surviving camp inmates as the war drew to a close were all too apparent.

It was at this juncture that the thought which was first voiced in Sachsenhausen—that we should beg Saint Joseph to rescue us—came up again. We commenced with ardent prayer preceding a solemn act of consecration to Saint Joseph's care in spiritual communion with his basilica in Kalisz (one of the best-known basilicas dedicated to Saint Joseph in the world). We then proclaimed the solemn act on Sunday, April 22, 1945. It was worded as follows:

Holy Joseph, chosen by God to be the guardian of Our Lord Jesus Christ and spouse of the Virgin Mary, Mother of God, receive this offering of our hearts and listen to the prayers we humbly address to you today.

The Holy Church and our fatherland are currently faced with new and exceptionally difficult historic challenges. Aware of this and trusting in your powerful intercession, we fly unto you, surrendering ourselves to your care, as your followers, united in the one faith, one love, and one mother-tongue, and now bound even closer together by our common prison-camp fate.

O holy patron of the holy Church, guardian of our fatherland, succor of families, just man who once carefully guarded and led the Child Jesus, we ask you to strengthen us and our whole nation in unfailing faithfulness to God and to the decrees of God's Church. Keep us true to social justice and love, and in the face of the dangers all around us, protect us, our cares, and our families, so that we may hastily return to our beloved country and work there in the cause of long sought-after peace.

Trusting in your intercession, we solemnly vow that on our successful return to our country:

We shall first, in deep understanding of your eminence, cultivate veneration of your person not only in our own hearts, but also at the same time, in our families.

Second, we shall give a common token of our thanksgiving in front of your miraculous image in the Kalisz Shrine a year after our return, whence we undertake to spread veneration of your name and respect for the precepts of social justice and love in our families, under the guidance of the Holy See, so that each of these should form a life-giving building-block of our dear country.

Third, as proof of our gratitude for our liberation we shall endeavor to bring about, so long as our means allow it, the birth of a new work of mercy in your name.

Holy Joseph, pray for us before the throne of the Most High God that these stirrings of our hearts should be for our own betterment, the good of our country, the flourishing of the Church, and the greater glory of Our Lord Jesus Christ. Amen.

It was a prayer for the rescue of men condemned to death, and also a prayer that our country and families be spared. It was an amazing prayer—one that resounded with faith and wisdom.

"The future of the Church and the nation is determined through the family," the Polish Pope later taught. There is no other future for the nation. In concentration camps, there were priests, the sons of Polish families, whose hearts were full of understanding for this truth. This was expressed even while they were face-to-face with the greatest of dangers so far, as the end of the enormous struggles of the Second World War came closer and closer.

One night at this juncture, sirens suddenly woke the camp to life: "Get up and stand in file outside your barracks!" We thought this must be a transport. . . . After all, these were the tactics employed when the Allies approached a camp: the prisoners would be ordered to march out onto a road which would first be marked by the execution of whoever could not keep pace, and then by the gradual extermination of others via exhaustion. (We were able to observe the survivors of marches from other camps who managed to reach Dachau, only to die here.)

That night, however, we observed a crowd of SS officers appear dressed in spotless non-combat uniforms. The drama of anticipation was mingled with the feelings that inevitably accompany the last moments of a giant tyranny's life. One prisoner commented: "Soon your pretty caps will fall from your heads." The prophecy was to be fulfilled very soon. Meanwhile, after a long wait, we were ordered back into our barracks!

Unbelievable! We were not going to be marched anywhere, even despite repetitive efforts to evacuate the camp.

Later we learned that, apparently, the intention had changed. We were not to be ordered to march out; rather, our case was to be "solved" on the spot. At the time, we failed to guess this SS policy, even when it began to be carried out. Time ran out, however, and the SS failed to carry out their plan of destruction before our liberators came on the scene.

This is how it happened:

On Sunday morning, April 29, 1945, the block chiefs were summoned to the camp command center where it was announced that the camp personnel had decided to retreat. The watchtowers were taken over by prisoners who served as guards in a very severe SS prison located right next to our camp. These prisoners were known as the "fallen angels." If anyone attempted to cross the barbed wire fence of the camp, he would be shot by them immediately.

Our block chiefs then returned, including our courageous Father Korcz. The announcement was passed on and comments were shared. Soon, we beheld the beautiful sights of a great white sheet being draped over the main camp gates, and smaller ones being hung from the watchtowers. Furthermore, the camp authorities were giving notice that they intended to surrender without battle.

16

You're Free!

The day was sunny and warm. Ardent prayers reverberated through the chapel. Holy Masses were being offered, and there was great anticipation. The hours passed slowly—very slowly.

Suddenly, we heard shouting. It started from the parade ground and spread through to all of the barracks. It was the shouting of thousands of prisoners going mad at the sight of the symbol of freedom: the Allied Forces. They were few in number, and it later became apparent how few. We heard gunshots. . . .

Behind the barbed wire of our block an American soldier was stealthily edging forward, quiet as a cat, in stark contrast to the loud soldier's march to which we had grown accustomed. Then another came along. Orders were given and the personnel of the watchtower descended. Then a series of gunshots brought them to death. That is how it went at all the watch towers. It turned out, despite the white flags that they had put up, that the SS officers in one of these towers still shot at the liberators—hence the retaliation.

An Allied contingent of scouts had already discovered the mountains of dead bodies that had neither been buried nor burnt for lack of time. The task of extermination had proved too great.

Meanwhile, shouts of incredible joy and relief reverberated throughout the camp. The national flags of all the countries represented were hung out on the barrack roofs. They appeared from nowhere, having been prepared earlier with much ingenuity, and well hidden until this moment.

Waves of prisoners—now ex-prisoners—ran down the Lagerstrasse for the first time in so many years without being chased on with "Los!" and "Schnell!" They celebrated the unique joy that only comes from newfound freedom. They surrounded an Allied soldier, probably the commander. He, too, shared in the joy of the liberated, and sent a celebratory shot from his handgun into the air.

Freedom: what a gift from God to man. Freedom: without which man cannot be man. Freedom: a necessity just like air and water and sunlight. Here was its unique manifestation—its unique experience.

The Allied commander entered the *Jourhaus* ("administration building") balcony, and trying to calm the survivors down, he shouted: "You're free! Thank God, not us. Whoever is able to pray, let him give thanks together with me!" He then made the Sign of the Cross and began reciting the "Our Father" prayer.

This was real freedom—the freedom of God's children! Freedom for all! And how much more so for those of us who already knew how to pray; who already knew that "Christ came to set us free!" *(Gal. 5:1)*; who believed that freedom was always and everywhere an option, and were finally experiencing it as God's visible, tangible, and sought-after gift—the image of His lasting gift of true inner freedom.

Even now after so many years have passed, I still have the ardent desire to be able to share that scene with all those, great and small (though always small!), who might be tempted to collaborate in compromising the personal freedom of others, and to sell themselves, disowning their own.

Meanwhile, in this now former camp, there came to be a threesome who finally stumbled upon the unusual idea: we're free, so let's run out into our freedom! The threesome included the Catholic priest Ignatius Jez, my great friend and Jesuit seminarian, Tadeusz Pelczar, and myself.

How often had we steeled our yearning glances from the distant greenery of meadows and woods? Would it still be possible to enjoy springtime before it passed? Either it was going to happen now, or it never would. Even though the Allies were here, the latter alternative still seemed more likely because the former had always been clouded in a fog of impossibility. Despite everything, though, the impossible became true, "For nothing is impossible to God." *(Lk. 1:37)*.

Thus, we ran out into the meadows and woods. En route we came across the relics of our immediate past, except this time it was SS officers rather than our fellow inmates that were lying dead from gunshots. In one of the Journaus windows we saw the stony face of our chief oppressor, Raportführer Betcher. He was surrounded by ex-prisoners; it must have been some type of lynch mob.

Was this just another link in the destructive chain? Can it not just be broken at last?

We arrived at the meadow and the woods right next to it as free men! Who could imagine anything more marvelous, or any more marvelous setting?

What gave us the idea? Perhaps it was our innate Polish attachment to the land and its beauty. O land, Polish land, may you be loved by all your children! Or, perhaps it was the same calling we are all born with, ever since God told Adam and Eve in the beginning: ". . . multiply, fill the earth and subdue it." *(Gen. 1:28)*. The calling is for man to be a wise steward of land; not a barbarian, thief, and occupier of it. It is for man to be a wise steward of the earth, which feeds all our brother men.

We stood in the meadow and looked back toward the camp. The sight was unbelievable! The setting sun revealed a thick cloud of dust rising above the camp. How could we have lived all those years in that tight space? There was a lot of commotion as we looked on, but such commotion had been a regular occurrence, especially during the parade ground assemblies and the marches out to work.

The area of the camp precinct was tight—very tight. It was astounding to think that it had recently accommodated more than 33,000 prisoners. That thought added yet another dimension to the inhuman picture of Dachau. We looked on, gazing at our past. We looked on with the eyes of all those who had lived there with us through so many years, and had either survived or fallen.

Soon night fell upon us. We were in the very same place and on the very same bunks, but oh, how different the atmosphere!

An unexpected noise interrupted our sleep. We heard the sounds of heavy fighting and gunshots. We were not surprised, though; after all, the war was still on. The battle sounds did not worry us, and that first night did not allow sleep, anyway. We remained oblivious to the fact that the prolonged fighting hid great danger from us. Only later did we find out that the battle was fought over us, over the camp. The SS still wanted to carry out the schedule of destruction that they had planned—they still hoped to leave only ashes.

Did the agents of destruction fall behind, or did the liberators make special haste? The latter was more accurate. According to the reports (which merit detailed examination), the Allied scouts had apparently reached the camp much earlier than the SS had expected.

One thing is beyond doubt: the oppressors were not capable of surrendering and simply allowing their victims to go free. That is probably always the case. It is very difficult to muster generosity when faced with one's own defeat; especially when earlier there had been no magnanimity to speak of in times of so-called success (even if only military). Successes do not mean victory if they ultimately inflict defeat—not on the vanquished, but on the vanquishers.

We experienced the adventure of freedom; and all the while our thoughts were occupied with the fact that freedom, to us, meant future.

In the short-term, what did the future hold in store for us? Typhoid outbreaks were still recurring in the camp, so for the time being, we had to be submitted to quarantine measures. We asked about the possibility of returning to Poland. For now, there was none. We just had to wait.

Some friends and I received instructions about how to get a post office system up and running. I thought the old SS offices might be suitable, so we went to visit them. We had never dreamed how enormous and ingenious the buildings erected around our camp actually were. The officers' buildings were yet another means of ensuring that any escape from camp would prove to be virtually impossible. It turned out that our häftlings' camp was surrounded not only by spacious barracks, but also by offices, houses, canteens, and restaurants. Many of them were underground—probably as a matter of taste and caution.

The buildings were almost luxurious, though by now they were almost completely devastated. They had been wrecked not by their ex-inhabitants who ran away, but by ex-prisoners who had already been through them. What a shame, I thought. Instead of wrecking them, they could have moved in to enjoy better human living conditions and some rest before returning home to conditions that could not be predicted.

My friends and I eventually chose a small, relatively clean building. There were four of us. We arranged some office and living quarters, including a dining room and a common bedroom. This comfort was unprecedented, at least according to the standards we had grown accustomed to. The nearby Allied kitchen supplied us with food, and the cook, an American sergeant of Polish descent, showed us particular favor. He treated us to a generous menu, but nevertheless we were still wary. The change in our circumstances was tied to the danger that our bodies, being so malnourished, could no longer cope with plenty. There were even cases of death recorded on this count.

After some weeks passed, a Vatican delegation from Paris came to the camp. The delegation was run by the unforgettable priest of the Order of Charity, Father Rodhain, who was then an army chaplain. It also included some Franciscan nuns—the Missionaries of Mary. They took care of the sick and dying with exceptional dedication, and even moved in to live with them, just across a partition wall. They also took shifts in adoration before the Blessed Sacrament, which was exposed around the clock in their simple quarters.

Thus it was that our time in camp came to an end. Edmund Michelet agreed, though not without difficulty (the economic situation in France being so poor), to take us to Paris, explaining that he did so out of regard for the seminarians who had waited so long for ordination. After various adventures associated with the journey (during which I found myself still suffering from the aftereffects of typhus, though enjoying the tender care of my faithful friends, especially Father Boleslaw Burian), we arrived in Paris very early one morning toward the end of May.

The exceptional architecture in the famous capital was almost untouched, but nonetheless, the city had been completely impoverished. Even so, we were warmly welcomed by its most venerable representatives: Cardinal Emmanuel Suhard, Archbishop of Paris, and the Papal Nuncio, Archbishop Angelo Giuseppe Roncalli (later Pope John XXIII), surrounded by other Church and lay dignitaries.

The meeting was an exceptional one, and further such encounters followed on from the first. Although enjoyable, our experience of these events was weighed down by the fact that we were in the midst of a period of difficult recovery, trying to recuperate both spiritually and physically. The years we had been through still weighed heavily upon us.

17

Phases of Freedom

Phases of freedom run largely parallel to the stages of enslavement engraved into the wartime history of Poland: into its hardships, its torments, and the enormity of its sacrifices.

Phases of freedom run in unison with sacrifice—including the sacrifice of life laid down by God's Church in our country during one of the richest periods in its history, the time of the Second World War.

Phases of freedom continue to progress to this day, with those past years as their backdrop.

Let me then recall, at least in a fragmentary way, the phases which have passed through to the present day.

I turn first to January of 1987. In Poland, the Eucharistic Year was just beginning, and the route for Pope John Paul II's third pilgrimage to our country was being planned. The Szczecin-Kamien diocese was entering into the fifteenth year of its recent re-establishment. It was a very young diocese, but nevertheless, it was greatly aware of its distinction as heir to the heroic missionary work of Saint Otto of Bamburg.[22]

In June of that same year, we were looking forward to the beatification of a second concentration camp prisoner patron saint: Blessed Michael Kozal, who had given up his life in Dachau forty-four years prior, on January 26, 1943.

What a grace-filled year!

How it was that I had survived long enough to be able to experience it still baffles me. Is there any answer other than that survivor's hymn sung in the Psalms: "Praise the Lord, for he is good, and his love is from age to age!" *(Ps. 107:1)*? Nothing is impossible to him. The Virgin Mary heard these words while standing on the threshold of her unique mission, and ever since Christ gave His last will and testament from the Cross we can run to her, because "never was it known that anyone who fled to her protection, implored her help, or sought her intercession was left unaided." These words, written by Saint Bernard in his prayer, "Memorare," have been counted on by innumerable hosts of men of all ages, including my own.

What was the inner meaning of the whole history of my concentration camp experience? What did it mean for the depths of my soul?

It was a great grace—one of the greatest of graces available. But why was this so?

I should not try to avoid answering this question, even though my certainty comes largely from faith. Witness in suffering cannot be surpassed by any other. It is given for the benefit of others, after all.

Let me mention the Apostle Paul's words to his disciple: "It is only on account of this that I am experiencing fresh hardships here now; but I have not lost confidence, because I know who it is that I have put my trust in, and I have no doubt at all that he is able to take care of all I have entrusted to him until that Day." *(2 Tm. 1:12)*.

Saint Paul then insists that such truths should be spoken with great humility: "So I shall be very happy to make my weaknesses my special boast . . ." *(2 Cor. 12:9)*.

The deepest motive is that of ardent thanksgiving: "If any one of you should suffer for being a Christian, then he is not to be ashamed of it; he should thank God that he has been called one!" *(1 Pet. 4:16)*.

Thus, boundless human weakness met the greatest of values for the ultimate goal of everything: God's glory. In fact, our God is boundless in his mercy. That is also why he wanted us to have a Mother of Mercy. Therefore, bearing in mind what was the most important dimension of what I have been privileged to experience, let me continue on to the consecutive phases of freedom which followed.

The first phase of freedom, as I have already mentioned, came in Paris, where we traveled to after those initial experiences of regained freedom while we were still in the precinct of the liberated camp. We were put up in a seminary in the Latin Quarter, rue du Regard 6. The main seminary building was outside Paris in Issy-les-Moulinaux. We were given the wing used by the seminarians in their final year.

Upon our arrival, we found Paris poverty-stricken. Our hosts, the Sulpician Fathers, did not allow us to feel the brunt of this; however, other inhabitants of the city failed to hide their displeasure when they learned that we were foreigners. They were hungry, and here were foreigners enjoying equal rights with French repatriates. On the other hand, we were also met with many gestures of good will. The country's legacy as "the Church's eldest daughter" was still in evidence, and we came to experience this on many occasions, even throughout our later lives.

Paris remained deeply imprinted on our memories: the capital city of a country allied with ours, which throughout history, extended hospitality to so many of our compatriots. Furthermore, it was the place where God ordained that we would receive our Holy Orders and commence our priestly lives.

We were transferred to *L'asyle de Nuit* , the night shelter for the poor at Rue Labat 44 at the foot of Montmartre hill and the Sacré-Coeur Basilica. We had had to leave our previous place to make way for its permanent inhabitants. This new locality was a poor one. Nights in the common hall proved sleepless for many of us; the hours of darkness ticked by while we listened to the chimes of Paris' numerous street clocks. (It is curious that the common concentration camp sleeping rooms allowed us to fall asleep easily.) Anyhow, that was the site Divine Providence chose as the place from which we would make our way, on July 29, 1945, to the Polish Church of the Assumption of Our Lady to become Christ's priests.

This happened two months after our arrival in Paris. We first had to take some additional exams and go through special retreats: first a common one led by Father Bieniasz (a great experience—our first retreat in freedom), and then a special one directly prior to our ordinations led by Father A. Wietrzykowski, the spiritual director of the Poznan seminary and companion to Cardinal Augustus Hlond through the war years.

After my ordination I made my way to the beautiful chapel of Saint Joan of Arc, which belonged to the Franciscan Sisters on Avenue Reille 36, and I offered my first Holy Mass. I then left to go to a health resort in Berck, off the English Channel coast, in northern France. There I had the chance to see the powerful defense fortifications built by the Germans on the seafront. They proved to be of no avail in the end, though. The preparations the Allies had to undertake to land on these beaches, however, were necessarily on a scale far surpassing anything known to history before that date. The barriers were a reflection of the enormity of the enemy's military machine, built up by a madman while the world looked on. What would have happened if he had managed to carry his schemes through to the end? How many more concentration camps would have appeared in Europe, and even around the world? Or rather, would the Third Reich instead just denote one great big camp? It is alarming to think that Europe reached the brink of such a precipice in the middle of the twentieth century!

We are all too well aware of how the situation in Europe has fluctuated since the Second World War. The end of the twentieth century could very well have heralded the destruction of the whole human race. Who would have defended us from such madness then? On October 27, 1986, our Pontiff, John Paul II, in Assisi, alongside representatives of the other world religions, turned to prayer and penance: "God is our refuge and our strength." *(Ps. 46:1)*.

The power that built the Atlantic fortifications also laid down multiple minefields in and among the coastal dunes. Toward the end, these were deposited in a totally haphazard way with no prior plans. Later I observed German prisoners of war employed in the mine-removal work—a difficult and dangerous task. Accidents were frequent, and often very grave. There arose the need for a priest who spoke German to attend to those workers, so I tried to be of service insofar as I could.

During my stay in Berck, the camp medical experimentation to which I had been subjected gave rise to more complications. I had developed a form of a bone disorder, but incredibly, specialist treatment for it was available at the resort. It was a curious coincidence, evidently choreographed by the eternal good God.

I later departed from Berck to undertake further studies at the University of Freiburg in Switzerland. After I completed my studies there in April of 1949, I returned home to Poland and to my diocese, which had suffered incredibly devastating wartime losses.

On my first day back, I was assigned to be one of the assistant priests in the large cathedral parish. I would be serving alongside the aged Father Joseph Kruszynski, a biblical scholar and former professor and rector of the Catholic University of Lublin, who was now parish priest. Little did I know at the time how important my experience there would turn out to be in my service to another diocese, the Szczecin-Kamien, which was also to suffer a serious shortage of clergy. In fact, the Szczecin-Kamien diocese is still suffering from priest shortages to this day.

Awhile later I was transferred to work at the Wloclawek Seminary. Its recent history of numerous martyrdoms drew new vocations like a magnet.

Later still, I was admitted to the grace of the fullness of the priesthood, the episcopacy, and was ordained bishop by Cardinal Wyszynski in the Wloclawek Cathedral. How things had turned since the time I bid farewell to this professor of mine, only to be later arrested in his very quarters! As bishop, I participated in the Second Vatican Council. Then, after a grave illness, I was forced to spend a period of recuperation in Sicily. Since I could visit Rome, I obtained my first private audience with Pope Paul VI. The subject of my meeting with the Holy Father, on that occasion, was my concentration camp experience.

The subject of the camps came up again when I submitted proposals to the Holy Father for a pilgrimage for priests and bishops who had been inmates of concentration camps to the sites of former prison camps, and ending in Rome during the 1970 golden anniversary of the Pope's priesthood.

The Vatican showed much enthusiasm for these pilgrimage plans: it was to be the first group pilgrimage from Poland to Rome in thirty years. Despite the enthusiasm, though, the Holy Father predicted that difficulties could arise, and he was not proven wrong. Even though prolonged negotiations with the Communist authorities about the matter seemed to be heading the right way, they concluded with a sudden verdict that the pilgrimage could not proceed due to lack of foreign currency.

Tensions escalated. The planned departure date was a few days after the Kalisz jubilee celebrations of April 29, 1970. These celebrations coincided with the twenty-fifth anniversary of Dachau's liberation, for which reason they included the consecration of a new chapel, the Chapel of Thanksgiving and Martyrdom in Saint Joseph's Kalisz Shrine. Meanwhile, the chance of success for the pilgrimage became increasingly slim. Nevertheless, I refrained from alerting the potential pilgrims to the problems because I was reluctant to give up on our plans.

Luckily in the end, it was a success after all!

Archbishop Sergio Pignedoli, a personal friend of Pope Paul VI, came to the rescue. He had come to Poland on a very short visit about some totally different matter, but ended up taking on our cause. Cardinal Wyszynski supported him in his efforts, and preached a fervent sermon in Kalisz. This could well be taken as the inauguration of the pilgrimage.

So, thanks to Saint Joseph's help, we set off on May 17, 1970.

The pilgrimage proved to be a very important event. Its schedule was very intense, and we had many important encounters. We were granted an audience with the Holy Father, and a meeting with Cardinal Albino Luciani—Patriarch of Venice and future Pope John Paul I. In Rome, the pilgrimage was headed by Cardinal Wojtyla, at Cardinal Wyszynski's request. This way we were able to meet not only the Pope, but two of his successors as well.[23]

Let me return to Dachau one more time: on visiting there in 1970, we failed to leave any mark of Polish witness. Thankfully we had bought a small commemorative plaque: a simple piece of stone with Polish and German inscriptions, which gave some key points of information concerning the Polish inmates of the ex-camp. We entrusted it to the care of Cardinal Julius Döpfner. However, it became clear that it was too small. It was necessary then, to prepare something more worthy of its function and to find a suitable place for it.

The site chosen was the outer wall of the chapel of Christ's Mortal Agony. A Warsaw artist named Benedict Tofil, the designer of the Chapel of Thanksgiving and Martyrdom in Kalisz, prepared a bronze cast of a design that had been approved by a special commission. A figure of the Sorrowing Christ (a typical Polish theme) was placed in the middle of the commemorative plaque. Four plates bearing inscriptions in four different languages that convey details of the numbers of Polish inmates, Polish priests, and others that laid down their lives surrounded it. The plaque was dedicated by the priest-inmates who had survived Dachau to all of their fellow prisoner-brothers whom they had to leave behind.

Once the design was completed, a group of us made our way to Munich and Dachau in order to erect the memorial in an official, ceremonious way (we hoped to achieve this before the 1972 Munich Olympic Games opened). Once there, we encountered several technical difficulties stemming from the fact that the chapel was built out of fieldstone. These difficulties were eventually overcome, though, thanks to the good will of Bishop Johannes Neuhäusler, and the architect in charge of the ex-camp. The Carmelite Sisters also greeted us with friendship, as always, and considered us especially close to their hearts. Thus, on Sunday, August 20, 1972, we offered Holy Mass in the Chapel of Christ's Mortal Agony, and the plaque was unveiled in the presence of Cardinal Döpfner and Bishop Neuhäusler.

Meanwhile, the Red Cross was commencing a research project on inmates living in Poland who had been subject to pseudo-medical experiments in concentration camps. Two representatives of the Bavarian Court were interviewing victims in the Warsaw Ministry of Internal Affairs. I agreed to a half-hour appointment, but the questioning dragged on . . . for seven hours. Finally, a Dr. Beyerlein from Munich asked me whether I would be willing to give testimony in court. I could not decline.

Therefore, in 1975, another phase of post-camp experience—of freedom—began. The Munich Courts were investigating the case of ex-Sturmbannführer Schütz, who had been responsible for the experimentation regimens in Dachau which I have already recounted. It was there that I was called upon to give witness.

Thanks to the kindness of Bishop Ernst Tewes, an auxiliary bishop of Munich, I was put up in a house just outside the city to prepare my testimony. The task, as I took it up, became harder and harder to fulfill, so on the evening before I was due to speak in court, I decided to put everything down on paper. The next day, the chief judge advised me not to use my notes, so I had them before me, but hardly referred to them as I testified in Polish.

I still remember well what I then wrote in detail as I prepared for my testimony, and I think it should be included here regardless of the repetition that it will entail:

Lord Justice!

I have divided my testimony into three parts: first I intend to describe the particular period of my camp internment when I was subject to medical experimentation; second I intend to describe the experiments themselves; and third and finally I will share why I consider it advisable, even imperative, to travel here to take part in these proceedings in the capacity of witnesses.

The period when I was singled out for experimentation:

Today marks exactly thirty-three years since the day I was singled out for the experimentation regime in Dachau, about which I am to give testimony.

It was 1942, the year I would say signified the worst abyss of dereliction I suffered throughout my whole dreadful camp life. There were an enormous number of mortalities that year—through malnutrition, hunger, and so called invalid transports to the gas chambers.

The whole hot summer was marked with work from dawn to nightfall (we would always get up before the sun even rose, with electric lights on), and the hunger that does not bear describing had its hold on most us for another year running. Autumn proved no easier for those who managed to survive. I had to continue to work in the crop fields, picking out gladiola bulbs from the saturated soil with my bare hands. It rained often, and our camp rags afforded no protection to us. It was bitterly cold.

It was in this year, on November 10, that after a whole day of work the chief Kapo of the infirmary, Zimmermann, visited our block. We were lined up in rows and he examined each of us in turn, choosing some without letting on what he was up to. I was among the ones he picked out. We anticipated that the exercise was probably related to the experiments, vague news of which had begun to spread through the camp some time ago. I anticipated the worst, so I entrusted all my affairs to my professor, Father S. Biskupski, a professor of Warsaw University.

The experiments I was subject to:

1. November 11, 1942 was the day the experiments began. It went as follows:

   (a) In the morning, after the parade ground assembly, the group of Polish clergy picked out the previous night was marched off to the infirmary. The whole day was taken up by medical examinations. Undressed completely, we had to wait around for hours for the individual examinations and their results. The exercise was intended to help them select twenty people from our group, eliminating those who were unfit for experiments because they were already too sick. I recall one case in particular: one prisoner who was suffering from some chest infection was eliminated. I mention this because it links in with the chest condition with which I was later to be diagnosed. I am ready to submit the relevant certification. Among the twenty who were finally chosen, there were two priests who were not Polish: Father Zamecnik, who was Czechoslovakian, and Pastor Tundermann, who was Dutch.

   (b) After completing the examinations, we were transferred to the first infirmary block, located in room three. There we had to draw lot numbers, which needless to say, were completely incomprehensible to all of us at the time. My card read, "18B." It later transpired that this meant I was to be part of the biochemical cohort.

(c) Evening fell. One by one my colleagues were led out of the hall. Eventually, I was taken too. I was led over to the operating theater and ordered to lie down on the table, at which point someone in an SS uniform injected a liquid material into my right thigh. I was later informed that the injection was 3 ml in volume.

(d) After the injection, a nurse led me back to room three. I heard muffled groans, and some of my colleagues who had been injected before me seemed delirious. The nurse then told me that the injection I had received was a very dangerous one, and that all the experiments would be harsh; he said the only factors that would allow me to pull through were a will to survive and faith that I could manage.

2. I quickly grew faint, and it was only with the utmost effort that I was able to get out of my bed for a few seconds around midnight. In the morning, when I was left sitting for a moment on the edge of my bed, I felt so faint that they had to lay me down immediately.

3. The illness I developed was worrying because it very rapidly became visible in the form of a very painful, bright red lesion. It ran down the lateral side of my right thigh, and drew the attention of the commission, who came daily to examine our progress. However, they did nothing to treat what they saw. Instead, they ordered me to wait for the day that they had already scheduled my operation for (which they described with the word: *"Inzision"*). Meanwhile, my colleagues and I were given some nondescript tablets. The pain was excruciating.

4. When the operation date arrived, the incision was performed. As I woke out of my anesthesia, I saw that my right leg was being dressed in stacks of tissue paper, and then being bandaged. My whole leg was placed on a rail. The next day, when my dressing was changed for the first time (which happened daily from then on), I saw two wounds on my leg from the incisions that had been made during the operation. Two rubber tubes ran through these incisions, and a lot of puss leaked from them. During the dressings the tubes were

removed, rinsed, and put back in place. The pain was dreadful, and so was the nervous tension.

In the beginning, all of this was done under water. Later, however, the same procedure was done in the ward itself. The pain was great—even when I would just lie still in bed. The slightest vibrations from the floorboards hurt dreadfully. I couldn't make any body movements without causing myself excruciating pain, and even my hand movements were very limited. I was in such a state that I found it extremely difficult to eat the normal camp rations we were given, despite my never-satisfied hunger. Nurse Hermann saw my pain, and gave me some analgesics once or twice.

5. This state of affairs began in early January of 1943. I was subjected to operations on two further occasions, one of which proved especially painful. Just before the third incision, when I was already laid out on the stretcher, I received the Sacrament of Extreme Unction.

Oberpfleger Stöhr, a man evidently harboring some good will toward us, made it clear that my state of health gave him cause for grave concern. I suspect this was because of the blood test results, which came regularly. With the help of a nurse named Franz, he transferred me, and put me under the care of Zdenek Zemecnik. He announced that I was on the brink of septicemia and that he would try to help me, even though the doing so could prove very dangerous because it went counter to the experimentation protocols. He gave me an injection (as far as I know, it was of Tibetin), and then he repeated the procedure on several other occasions. To the surprise of all my friends, I got better quite rapidly. The whole rescue operation had to be kept under utmost secrecy; it was only possible thanks to the fact that the commission stopped visiting our ward out of fear of the typhoid fever outbreak which had just hit the camp. I eventually left the ward that April, after haveing spent about three months there.

6. During the experiments, seven out of our group of twenty died. Father Zemecnik died in the first few days, as did another Polish priest whose surname I cannot recall. I was especially grieved at the departure of a young teacher in the Oblates' seminary, Father Dr. Joseph Kocot. His bed was directly adjacent to my own, so I was the closest witness of his dreadful suffering prior to his death. Pastor Tundermann was similarly laid out on a stretcher

just in front of me so that an SS doctor could be shown how his whole body had turned completely yellow. I recall how the doctor then asked which group he belonged to, and how, on hearing that it was Group B, the biochemical group, he forbade anyone from helping him. Tundermann died shortly afterward.

Father Czeslaw Sejbuk, a Jesuit from Warsaw and editor of *Misja Katolicka*, among others, also died in agony due to bed sores, after having been through multiple incisions. The ones who suffered the most frequent incisions were Father Stanislaw Wolak, a Capuchin monk, who died not long ago in Australia, and Father Steven Baczyk, who gave his testimony here but a few days ago. Several also died shortly after the war, including Monsignor Leopold Bilko, Father Marian Suski, and Father Henry Dembrych.

As for those few still alive today, I recently heard from our bishop that the state of Father Stepien's health precludes his coming to give testimony here. I too, were it not for the special help and care I have been afforded, would not have been able to come here for health reasons even though I was the youngest of those on the experimentation ward.

7. In 1945, also in Dachau, I suffered a serious bout of typhus, again, in especially difficult circumstances. The experiments I had been subjected to were not taken into account at all, and I was given no special care. When Franz Y. saw me as a convalescent on a ward of typhus survivors he could not believe his eyes. I had managed to pull through this additional illness after what I had suffered a few years before. Even though he was not a believer himself, he said my survival could only be attributed to God. Nonetheless, when I left camp at age twenty-nine, I was hardly fit for life.

8. Although the present court proceedings only concern one man, Herr Schütz, I must mention that the whole commission carried out the experiments. Indeed, the SS-Sturmbannführer Schütz headed the commission, but here in court is the first time I've ever seen the defendant appear alone. I can still hear the announcement scream of Herr Stöhr, which we heard daily: *"Sturmbannführer Schütz kommt!"* It always meant that the whole commission was coming, though, including one man in civilian dress who was said to be a professor from Berlin. However, it is true that the commission was headed by the Stumbannführer Schütz. That was indeed the case.

9. Herr Schütz, as well as his companions, did not look upon us as sick patients needing medical assistance and the most basic of care; instead, they exclusively saw us as guinea pigs. During the most difficult period for us, we were even deprived of the camp rations which normally applied even to the sick. We also were not exempt from standing at attention whenever the SS entered our ward. I cannot recall Herr Schütz ever showing us any signs of human consideration. He was only interested in the research protocol, with his secretary taking down every word he dictated.

10. On the other hand, I assumed (and my colleagues probably thought the same) that after the experiments ended, yet another commission would come and condemn us to the gas chambers. There was one day when Herr Stöhr also expected the arrival of such a commission. Fortunately, it proved to be a false alarm.

11. After liberation somebody brought me my file from the camp office, which was supposed to have contained my camp documentation. However, except for the first page (the personal data taken down in Sachsenhausen), all of the remaining records had been torn out and destroyed. I have the little that was left here with me for the court's use.

12. After the liberation I was also informed about a fragment of the reports concerning the experiments we underwent. It included mention of the fact that they proved futile even from the purely scientific point of view.

13. I am also in possession of official medical reports on the state of my health. It seems to be the case, however, that for the purpose of the court what is most important is that I give an accurate account of the experiments I underwent.

Why have I agreed to come and give my testimony at these proceedings?

1. I did not come here to testify out any motive of hatred or revenge. Let me repeat that these proceedings are an exceptionally demanding experience for me; in a sense they represent the continuation of my sufferings on the experimentation wards. Even so, I have forgiven everybody, and I have even included words of forgiveness in my last will and testament, in view of the fact that

death is always possible. I am, after all, an advocate of peace and reconciliation, and I have shown that many times both in my private life and in my public ministry, as well as under the aegis of the Polish Bishops Conference and its famous letter of reconciliation addressed to the German Bishops Conference during the Second Vatican Council.

2. The obligation to care for social harmony and order is, however, universal. The basic principle of such a social order is the human person's sacred right to life—from conception in the mother's womb to natural death. International declarations, after all, emphasize the same.

I spoke about this during the Second Vatican Council in the name of all Polish bishops.

3. The doctor's oath and the very nature of the medical profession should guarantee that the doctor is there to heal, not to maim or kill.

4. My testimony is something I owe to those who laid down their lives. Among the very many Polish inmates, Polish clergy represented a special sizable group at Dachau. They were also subjected to particular persecution. The Dachau experimentation wards were one of the witnesses to this fact. According to Dr. Theodore Musiol, the malaria experiments were also carried out largely on Polish clergy.[24] In regard to the inflammation experiments I underwent, it was said that the first cohort was comprised of Jews, the second professional criminals, and among the twenty members of our third group, eighteen were Polish priests, with the fourth group comprised solely of Polish clergy.

The experiments about which I testify here, therefore, include only part of the wider picture. The statistics are as follows: among the 2,720 priests of twenty different nationalities at Dachau, 1,780 were of Polish extraction, and half of them died in the camp. Among all the remaining nationalities approximately 18 percent lost their lives. There were 223 priests from my diocese alone in Dachau, and among them, 148 died there. Among those who died were my seminary tutors and professors, and our bishop, my predecessor, the Venerable Michael Kozal. He died while the experiments were being carried out on us, in the same infirmary I was in, by a lethal injection on January 26, 1943.

From my diocese, only a handful of us are still alive, and only a few remain from among all the dioceses and religious institutions who can still give witness to the atrocities we experienced. Perhaps God has granted that we are still alive today so that we might bear witness to those who died. I am now witnessing for those who laid down their lives in the course of the medical experiments in the Dachau infirmary—the ones who were with me in group three of the Kunstphlegmone Research Program.

Such was the testimony I gave to the Munich Court, not far from Dachau. It was meant more as a witness than a testimony. Every witness to truth should also serve the purpose of peace-building and reconciliation. There is no other way to build a better future, other than basing it on truth. It may be an uphill struggle, but it is the only way.

My experience giving witness was a difficult one. The courtroom saw many dramatic events unfold in those hearings. Some of the witnesses suffered breakdowns under the pressure of recollections awakened by the searching questions. However, no one seemed to care about their welfare. Both the press and society at large showed scant interest, but then, when I tried to stretch my hand out to the defendant as a sign of forgiveness, some sort of awakening happened.

Cardinal Döpfner personally kept himself up to date on all the details of the case. He asked me to give him a personal account of my own. Once again, he exhibited much good will and courtesy, just as he had at our previous encounters in Dachau and Munich in 1970 and 1972.

I never anticipated that this would be the last time I ever saw the Cardinal, because his demeanor at the time did not show any signs of physical ailment at all.

Then the *Katholische Nachrichten-Agentur* ("Catholic News Agency," herein KNA), and Bavarian Television invited me for interviews. After some hesitation, I eventually agreed to both. They were recorded in the KNA center. The center's director, Dr. Norbert Stahl, expressed indignation at the indifference of the German mass media in regard to the court proceedings. I then watched as one interview was transmitted on the evening news. My interviewer introduced me, and emphasized that I appeared unwell. This was not too far removed from the truth, even though, thankfully, as a Polish bishop, I could enjoy good medical care, whereas other witnesses had no access to any medical services to speak of. However, my own companions privately endeavored to help them as much as possible.

On my return to Poland, Cardinal Wyszynski received me to hear my account of the proceedings. He asked me to prepare a report for the Plenary Bishops' Conference, so I did, and the Conference Proceedings mention it.

My report was then published in the weeklies: *Tygodnik Powszechny* ("Universal Weekly") on March 14, 1976, and *Gosc Niedzielny* ("Sunday Visitor") on March 28, April 4, and April 11, 1976. In addition, the journal *Chrzescijanin w Swiecie* ("The Christian in the World") printed the full unabridged text of my testimonies, to which I had sworn to on November 11, 1975. It also published a detailed analysis of the entire proceedings by Henry Wuttke, in an article entitled "The West German Press on Proceedings against an SS Medical Practitioner from Dachau."

The indifference of public opinion stood in stark contrast to how we, the witnesses and victims, experienced the proceedings. On November 6, 1975, the KNA reported: "What is most striking about the circumstances of these Munich Court proceedings is the almost total lack of public interest shown in regard to the circumstances in which the priest martyrs of Dachau laid down their lives."

The trend in Germany was clearly to forget. The same papers which so often wrote about Polish affairs now proved completely oblivious to the proceedings—to draw attention to them would undermine their assumptions.

The truth is that a similar lack of public interest was also a problem among the Poles. Why? Hadn't it been a detriment to society?

On March 1, 1979, during the first year of his pontificate, Pope John Paul II entrusted me—I was then the auxiliary bishop of Wloclawek—with the Diocesan See of Szczecin. The revived diocese of Szczecin-Kamien is now fulfilling its mission in the border territories along the banks of the Oder River and the Baltic Sea coastline. Cedynia, which centuries ago was witness to battles waged by Kings Mieszko I and Boleslaw Chrobry, is the western-most town on the Oder River. To the North, in the Baltic coast regions are Wolin, the seat of the first bishopric in the region, Swinoujscie, on the Uznam Island, and Kamien, which in its day was the seat of more than thirty consecutive bishops.

Not far from Cedynia lies Siekierki—the site of the dreadful struggles that ensued before the madman in Berlin finally surrendered. Sachsenhausen is nearby.

All of this has a deeper significance. During our survivor's pilgrimage in 1970, Cardinal Wojtyla spoke at the Monte Cassino cemetery of how two large categories of survivors returned to Poland after the war: soldiers from the battlefields and prisoners from the concentration camps. His words were:

And in this way soldiers set forth from the Polish lands, lands in distress, and via various routes, through various countries and parts of the world, made their way here: not only here, but also here. And priests also set out in the footsteps of these soldiers. They continued to be shepherds, just as in times of peace. This fact is of historical significance. Alongside this group, hosts of prisoners also set out from Poland on their journeys—but these were not journeys for freedom and to battlefields, but of imprisonment, of humiliation so deep, as only man is capable of inflicting on another. Priests, and these in vast numbers, were also among this second group. These were the two historical categories of men displaced from our country, and although their ways never crossed so long as the war lasted—each being in a different direction and having a different purpose—it is still true to say that both these groups marched together in one common cause.

Thus, my priestly ministry as a past inmate of nearby Sachsenhausen and faraway Dachau continues on the Oder and Baltic coasts. The Primate of the Millennium, Cardinal Wyszynski, in whose apartment I was first arrested and imprisoned as a Wloclawek seminarian, later wrote in a letter to mark my installation as the second bishop of the revived Szczecin-Kamien diocese the following telling words:

I express my great joy at this honoring of Your Lordship, this elevation to the episcopal seat of Szczecin-Kamien. All the more so since fulfilling your apostolic mission, my dear Bishop Kazimierz, as an ex-concentration camp inmate, as the victim of such inhuman sufferings, torments, and humiliations during the last terrible war, you should become a living testimony for our country to the justice of the Father of Nations, and a warning to other peoples!

I pray that I may fulfill this mission of mine always, for the sake of building a Civilization of Love.

On July 6, 1984, I spoke in Dachau during the Munich *Katholikentag* ("Catholics Day"):

I shall repeat what I said two years ago in Flossenbürg: the work of reconciliation must now be taken further. . . . Every sign of Christian love we extend to each other is as yet another brick in that great edifice of unity, peace, and Christian renewal of Europe. In the year 1000 A.D., Emperor Otto III made his way to Poland, accompanied by papal legates, to lay down the foundations of a new Christian order. Now, with the year 2000 dawning, could not—or rather should not—this new Christian order return among us? Germans and Poles—two central-European Christian nations—ought not only be reconciled with each other, but ought also enjoy good mutual understanding and show each other mutual love in the name of Christ, our Lord. It is high time!

A week before the meeting in Dachau, on the feast of Otto III of Bamberg, I consecrated a church dedicated to the Oder Queen of Peace in the parish of Siekierki. How much her help and succor is needed around the world, not least in this area of the Oder and the Baltic coast. We are right to entrust ourselves to this help of hers: the succor of the Queen of Peace and the Mother of the Prince of Peace who "made peace by his death on the Cross." *(Col. 1:20)*. Our neighbors, too, should consecrate themselves to her, together with all the nations of the world. To put our trust in her is to take heed of her plea: "Do as Jesus tells you." *(cf. Jn. 2:5)*.

The fortieth anniversary of the revival of the Church's mission in Szczecin—a difficult mission representing the fruit of the exceptional sacrifices made by a nation condemned to annihilation, as well as the fruit of the struggles of history's worst war to date, the Second World War—was dedicated to the care of Mary, the Mother of the Church and the patroness of the diocese. Next to her image there stands a statue of Saint Otto, co-patron of the diocese.

We also sought the intercession of Saint Jadwiga of Slask.[25] Her courageous son Henry met his death on the Oder in defense of Christianity, and she, herself, is the patron saint of reconciliation between nations.

Europe, as a whole, has recently gained new patrons: Saint Benedict, Saint Cyril, and Saint Methodius.[26] They, too, are all too fit to be patrons of peace-building and reconciliation: Cyril and Methodius were apostles to the Slavs, though they, themselves, were not Slavs. They underwent many torments on account of their witness to Christ, a witness that contradicted human ambitions.

Reconciliation and love: aims which constantly stand before us; targets to be achieved through hardship. It becomes all the more clear that "our help is in the name of the Lord." *(Ps. 124:8)*. With us, in intercession before him, we have our patron saints. "Let us conquer evil with good"—with their help!

On September 23, 1972, in the chapel of the ex-concentration camp in Flossenbürg, I had an encounter with German clergy. It found its echo not only in the hearts of all the participants who were ex-inmates, but also in those who were not. I have experienced the same in Germany time and time again, as I could never keep silence about my past experiences there. One must never hide the truth, though it should always be conveyed with love: *"Facientes veritatem in caritate."* ("Professing the truth with love.") *(cf. Eph. 4:15)*.

In Flossenbürg, I had to preach from my wheelchair. Soon after, though, I had an operation in Mallersdorf. Perhaps that small amount of suffering of mine was necessary? Yes—sacrifice is never futile. Its price, however, is carried by all of us: every son and daughter of Poland, this distressed nation of ours. This should not, on any account, lessen our sensitivity to the suffering of other nations. It should not make us one-sided. One-sidedness does not convey the truth and is unjust. I beg you to let no one harbor it.

Thus, we should be looking toward a Civilization of Love: "Love takes no pleasure in other people's sins but delights in the truth." *(1 Cor. 13:6)*. "If we live by the truth and in love, we shall grow in all ways into Christ, who is the Head." *(Eph. 4:15)*.

In testifying to the sanctity of all the Polish priests whose deaths I witnessed so close at hand, I would also like to mention that I have been called to give testimony in the beatification process of Father Carl Leisner, and I have also given testimony on behalf of Father Joseph Kentenich. "Professing the truth with love. . . ."

The act of consecration to Saint Joseph that we pronounced as prisoners at one of the most dangerous moments we ever faced, also gave expression to a deep solicitude for the fate of the institution of the family. It is this very concern (permeating the Church in Poland) that has given rise to the creation of an educational institute dedicated to modern family issues. The intention was to work together to develop the theology of marriage and the family, and relate it to studies in other disciplines of learning—all with the overall goal of building up support for the family. The plan, which broke new ground and also proved very difficult, was entrusted to the guidance of Saint Joseph. Then, counter to all expectations, the authorities communicated their agreement to carry out our plan to us on April 29, 1975. I received the message in Kalisz, in Saint Joseph's Basilica, during celebrations marking the thirtieth anniversary of the liberation of Dachau.

That was how the Institute for Studies on the Family was founded. Its basic assumptions have since found confirmation in the apostolic exhortation of John Paul II, entitled "Familiaris Consortio," which speaks of the need to organize higher education in family studies to underpin the Church's pastoral role in relation to the family. Throughout its existence and development, the Institute has consistently borne witness to the unfailing help of Saint Joseph, the Guardian of the Holy Family of Nazareth, and it is a reflection of the undertakings we made as prisoners in Dachau.

So far, I have outlined the main public events that I took part in following my camp experiences. Let them speak for themselves. Let them give witness.

I should also recall a whole series of more private encounters— beginning with those at the University of Freiburg in Switzerland when two German students who were departing upon completion of their studies, thanked me for always showing kindness to them, and for using the German language without prejudice. Could I have done otherwise? I wanted the new times to unfold in a new spirit: one not responding with evil, but with good—and this forever, from camp days on.

I also experienced another series of more official encounters with representatives of the Jewish nation. Such encounters were almost non-existent in the camp itself. We would not have found them difficult, though, because we all came from an environment where we met Jews on a daily basis. However, there was a double barrier set between us by the camp regime: that of language (we never met any Jews from Poland), and that which came from the particularly grievous persecution that both we as Polish clergy, and they as Jews, experienced, but which only lessened any chances of our keeping in touch with one another even further. In addition, the Jews disappeared from our camp life relatively quickly. We saw them in Sachsenhausen and again in Dachau, but both times it was only in the initial phases.

Nevertheless, on account of my concentration camp experiences, I later met up with Jews on two occasions in an official capacity.

The first was organized by the Jewish community in Rome after their synagogue suffered a terrorist attack on October 9, 1982. The meeting took place in the presence of Archbishop Bronislaw Dabrowski, Secretary to the Polish Bishops' Conference, and Monsignor Stanislaw Jezierski, a former camp inmate. During the official program, I delivered an address which was then responded to by Rabbi Vittorio della Rocca, whose father, Rubino della Rocca, had died in a concentration camp. It was Rabbi Vittorio who was presiding at a religious service in the Rome synagogue at the time of the attack. Then, after the official addresses were over, I went to visit all of the wounded people who were in a hospital on Saint Bartholomew's Island. The whole meeting proved very memorable.

The second such occasion was on April 18, 1983, when I represented the Polish Bishops' Conference in celebrations marking the reopening of the Warsaw synagogue. My address on this occasion included the following excerpt:

> There must be something of an innate greatness in man if the Pentateuch of Moses says: "So God created man in his own image and likeness." *(Gen. 1:27).*
>
> The same is true of every man—every brother of mine.
>
> The same is true also of all the Jews whom I still have before my eyes from the time we spent together in that abyss of death which is known as the concentration camp.
>
> The same is true, too, in regard to the Jewish children whom I have constantly before my eyes, and whose voices I can still hear: those Jewish children from the Baltic States, whom I once met on the camp Lagerstrasse as they marched to their merciless ends.
>
> The same is true of all those who died in those dreadful days of the uprising and extermination of the Warsaw Ghetto forty years ago.
>
> I pray together with Pope John Paul II, turning my thoughts to my Jewish brothers and sisters, wherever they met their cruel deaths: "May the Eternal Lord accept their offering for the redemption of the world" (John Paul II, April 13, 1983).

18

Witness or Confession?

everything I have recounted in this book is only a shortened version of my experiences. My memory made the selections, with some help from my human psychology, as well. My wartime experiences were difficult, and recalling them has also proved testing. Someone once wrote: ". . . and now I fear my own dreams," which can also mean, "I fear my own recollections." However, nothing can be done about this. Distance in time is of no assistance—actually, the opposite might very well be the case.

On departing from Dachau, I remember thinking that from then on there would be no more room for fearing anyone or anything. That was an illusion; the fear remains, and perhaps has even grown over time—especially when I visit the ex-camps. The fear remains, but it must not be allowed to take over one's humanity. It is an experience that is given to us in order to allow us to become more human, not the other way around. It is given to us so that the precept and virtue of courage and fortitude do not remain empty phrases.

This is why Christian martyrdom is so difficult: Christian fortitude has to endure everything, however great the fear. The *Acta*

Martyrum ("Acts of the Martyrs"), the official records of the trials of early Christian martyrs made by the notaries of the court, consists of examples of the most difficult witnesses to Christ that have ever been given.

After the war, a chapel was erected in Dachau and dedicated to the *Todesangst Christi* ("Mortal Agony of Christ"). The dedication was one that had never appeared anywhere else—but here, it was very appropriate. Christ Our Lord Himself was present in the fear and victory of his disciples. However, before it came to this, He had already shown us the way in the Garden of Olives in Gethsemane, when He "began to feel sorrow and distress" *(Mt. 26:37)* as His own passion began. Above all, though, resound the words of His prayer: "Father, let thy will not mine be done." *(Mt. 26:39)*.

My intent, however, is not to witness to apostles of Christ carved out of stone. That would be no witness at all. Those were all real witnesses given by real men who followed their Sorrowful Master. Rather, it is ultimately my obligation to give testimony to the living witnesses I saw. Let me do this for the Glory of God, who worked so powerfully through these brothers of mine. As I have already mentioned, quoting Saint Paul: "If anybody should suffer as a Christian . . . let him praise God on this account!"

This is the "confession" I must make, and I have done so in these reflections. I am entitled to make it, even though I am not a Saint Augustine. There is no other way in which I can provide the required witness.

On my return from the Munich Courts in 1975, Cardinal Wyszynski said the following words to me: "I knew it would be difficult, but it was an obligation." Indeed, the whole ordeal did turn out to be harder than I expected. The claims of the defense lawyers humiliated and appalled us. We also felt powerless before the reluctance of contemporary opinion to face up to the reality of past atrocities.

It is difficult, after all, to confront reality honestly if it entails truths that cannot be communicated. No one who has not personally experienced the reality of what I have tried to describe can ever fully understand it; they must remain men untouched in their depths by such awesome experiences.

Despite all of this, though, the obligation to give witness still stands.

I recall how Cardinal Seper, within the precincts of a former concentration camp, once admonished a group of young people that it was inappropriate for them to sing and dance in such a place. I remember how they reacted with surprise. I also remember how the man who was my driver from Munich to Dachau asked me if I would be interested in visiting the Order of the Carmelites there, because he had heard something about them once. When I mentioned, however, that their convent was located within the grounds of a former concentration camp, he expressed astonishment. He knew nothing of the camp. It was unbelievable, but I had to accept it.

Thus, there is an obligation to convey information and historical truths, an obligation all the more grave when historical truths are being neglected or lost in silence. The report I delivered after I testified in Munich Court was informative and telling, but it did not, by any means, fully satisfy the need.

Witness is also something I owe to my country, a land that was headed for destruction. This condemnation of Poland should be explored from all angles. It deserves to be remembered. Such historical memory should not only enrich our own national experience but should also help to secure justice on a wider front, whether European or worldwide. We have worked hard over the last thousand years to gain such justice, and no one could have foreseen what sacrifices would be required in the wake of the second millennium!

I also hope that this witness might become a small asset in the treasury of the Church; that Church so intimately bound up with the history of our country, but at the same time, universal in all its dimensions.

Father Maximilian Maria Kolbe was the first to enter into the *Martyrologium Romanum*[27] as a holy martyr of our century—the first to be recognized among concentration camp martyrs.

Like all martyrs, these companions of mine were also witnesses to Christ. The merciful Lord allowed me to behold their sacrifices firsthand, with my own eyes, and to remain alive so many years later. It must, without a doubt, be my solemn duty to give evidence of their witness.

The time for me to provide this witness, this confession, is now.

Epilogue

It is right that lessons should be drawn from history. Let us draw, therefore, from the extraordinary events that unfolded during the past century: an extraordinary century in Polish history. Let these events teach us by their example.

The first two decades of the twentieth century represented a time of preparation. Poland was getting ready to regain its independence after a long period of foreign rule. Freedom did not come until after immense sacrifices had been made by Poland as a nation, though: attempts at insurrection; imprisonments and miserable deportations to Siberia; *Kulturkampf* ("cultural struggle") struggles to keep the Polish language alive; and battles to reclaim every inch of Polish land.

Poland's independence had earlier been extinguished in the wake of the May 3, 1791 Constitution, which reawakened the envious hatred of our neighbors. Many years later, though, Poland was once again set to appear on the world's maps as a consequence of the First World War (1914–1918). It was this war that opened our twentieth-century history. Poles, in line with the invocation, "For your freedom and ours," took part in it on all fronts.

The aftermath of the First World War heralded the revival of Polish independence after decades of struggling and suffering. It was revived by the forces of spirit that were unfailingly nurtured by the work of the nation's poets, the writings of great authors, and the genius of Chopin. There were uprisings, but ultimately, this revived independence derived from our cultural traditions faithfully preserved around the Polish family hearth.

Before the first two decades of the twentieth century drew to a close, however, the young, independent republic had to embark on a new and urgent war effort, because the Red Army onslaught was approaching from the East. The whole nation, inspired to bravery and selflessness, quickly formed tight ranks that even included scouts and other youth volunteers. Across the oceans and in Western Europe, the Polish émigré community also tightened ranks to form the Blue Army.

Things came to a head in August of 1920. In the outskirts of Warsaw, Poland saw one of its greatest victories—shattering a power that carried the banner of war against God and His Mother, the Virgin Mary and Queen of Poland. It came to be known as the Miracle at the Vistula. This great battle of 1920 saved Warsaw and Poland, and also rescued Europe—a feat accomplished by Poland for by no means the first time in history. Furthermore, Poland had once again managed to do it at the very dawn of its revived independence.

The following two decades proved to be a time of unbelievably rapid reconstruction and reorganization of the country. Gdynia and its modern sea harbor were built from scratch, which meant that Poland's long-awaited access to the coast could be exploited without restraint. A Central Industrial Circuit was then developed in another poor region of the country, Stalowa Wola. The whole country saw the rapid development of a broad spectrum of building programs. Schools and education institutes of different types and levels were founded, and Spiritual and material culture both flourished.

Before these two decades ended, though, Germany and the heir of Russia, the Soviet Union, sealed an alliance. These two neighboring powers, this time under the rule of the two greatest tyrants of the twentieth century, Adolf Hitler and Joseph Stalin, engulfed Poland once again.

Thus, the Second World War, started by Hitler's sudden attack on Poland on September 1, 1939, broke out. Stalin and his army quickly joined in. Once again, the Polish people embarked on a heroic struggle, fighting bravely in the Underground Army and on all European fronts, from Narvik to Monte Cassino, as well as in the extraordinary Warsaw Uprising. These struggles were accompanied by the inhuman suffering of the whole nation. As the regime of terror intensified, their extermination plans were systematically executed, but in such a way as to not lose too much slave labor too quickly. The extermination process of the Polish population was slower than that of the Jewish population, which was carried out with infernal haste.

Terror reigned to the East and West, and was the instrument of the Civilization of Death. Poles were most affected to the East—there the terror was manifested in the village of Katyn, where Soviet authorities ordered the mass execution of Polish military officers, policemen, and civilian prisoners.

Soviet *gulags* ("labor camps"), were another mark of extensive persecution, and were filled with innumerable Poles. The gulag network was akin to Hitler's concentration camps, and the total number of both is difficult to count. Of these, Dachau, located in Bavaria not far from Munich, was the first to be built, and was the scene of the oppression of Polish clergy and faithful.

The inmates of gulags and concentration camps became somewhat of an army in their own right, and defended Poland alongside the Underground Army, the Polish Armed Forces, and the Warsaw Insurrectionists. They came into formation first in the West, and then also in the East. The prisoners defended Poland with as much bravery as those on the outside, just in a different way. It was of these brave prisoners that the then Cardinal Karol Wojtyla spoke of at Monte Cassino in 1970 (quoted in Chapter 17, page 152). It is not possible, before God and man, to evaluate or measure the total contribution toward freedom afforded by this innumerable host of prisoners: those who made for a free Poland through passion, terror, and death.

You Shall Be My Witnesses is a witness to my own prison experiences. It is meant as a representation of what was but a drop in the ocean of the suffering experienced by all Poles during the Second World War. Its story, however, is typical of twentieth-century Polish history, because evil is not creative, and always implicit to it is the horrid mark of rebellion against God, and of disregard for man. Evil always tries to appear under the guise of law, but it does so dressed in the lies and cruelty of the Civilization of Death.

Freedom returned to Poland shortly before the middle of the century, but it was a very tenacious freedom, and excesses committed under Communism not long ago are still being chronicled.

The twentieth century finally ended with a chain of wars erupting throughout several continents—the last one in the Balkans, right on Poland's doorstep. What happened to the solemn declarations for peace forged by the world international organizations? Has mankind in this century lost track of the right to peace—that is to say, the right to life?

We have just recently celebrated a series of anniversaries of great events: the Nuremberg trials, the Universal Declaration of Human Rights, and the Atlantic Pact. What have these distinguished events, all resulting from the experiences of the Second World War, contributed? Have we been able to forestall the return of additional atrocities? Where are we heading? These questions are just, but difficult. An address entitled, "An Attempted Conclusion—The Way Ahead," that I delivered on December 1, 1998 at the closure of a symposium sponsored by the Pontifical Academy for Life, represented an attempt at some answers.

Which way are we heading—for or against life? That is a question on which man's very existence depends. An eminent demographer who spoke at the twenty-eighth International Family Congress in Warsaw has published a well-documented paper carrying the eloquent title: "Europe Is Dying Out." In it, the chances ahead for Europe and the European Union are evaluated in various ways. Is it known, however, that above and beyond all the other forecasts there looms one of Europe's demise? The publisher of that paper notices that "no one is speaking out about it. . . ." Moreover, Poland is dying out—who is speaking out about that? Apparently, the European Union wishes Poland's population was half its present size. Can anybody explain this?

It is imperative to speak of this. It is important to identify the Civilization of Death for what it is, and to counter the maddening propaganda machine that is almost universally spread by the mass media. In addition, if there are any media at the service of the Civilization of Love, they ought to be placed on a pedestal among our greatest achievements.

Which way should we be moving? We should be moving in the way of Truth. "The truth shall set you free." *(Jn. 8:32).*

A great effort is needed to convince people in our rather decadent twentieth-century cultural circles that they ought to choose the blessing of life, not the curse of death; that they should look with favor not on the murderer Cain, but on the noble Abel; and that they ought to rejoice in the truth and joy that "another man has been born into the world" *(cf. Jn. 16:21),* not that the mother never heard the silent scream of her own child killed in her womb.

Instead, however, a great effort is being expended to convince man that the Civilization of Death has great appeal and affords good prospects for the future. Hedonism, consumerism, lust of the body, and fascination with evil all serve to oil the gears of the Civilization of Death.

Is it, therefore, true to say that the inspired words: "Conquer evil with good," have lost their power? Are we allowed to admit thoughts to ourselves that God's grace is no longer omnipotent? Or that two-thousand years after his coming into the world, Christ's words, which have been unceasingly repeated by the Church, have lost validity—those words which assure us "your sins are forgiven, go and sin no more"? *(Lk. 5:20; Jn. 8:11).*

He said, "You shall be my witnesses." *(Acts 1:8).* Are we?

Which way should we proceed? Let us go in the way of Christ's witnesses, right through to the ends of the earth *(Acts 1:8)*, though first to all the corners of our own country.

"The family is the way of the Church," preaches Pope John Paul II. Without this "community of love and life," there shall be no true life for man, nation, Church, and humanity.

So which way should we proceed? We should proceed in the way of the family; decisively, ardently, and wisely.

Lastly, we must return man to God. Left to his own devices, man will never save himself. Without God he will die mercilessly at the hand of man—man who has rebelled against God. Man alone, without God, is capable of inflicting on his fellow man that which he has already done toward the end of the first half of the twentieth century, and continues to now at an ever-growing pace. Man has become both victim and oppressor in one.

Which way should we be heading? We should be heading toward the God of Life—toward the God of every man's life.

Return man to God, and welcome man as coming from God's hand. God is Creator and Father of every man. Do not say: "Let there be some exceptions, there must be some." Do not say that, because every man's life, no exceptions made, carries the price paid by Cain.

I have been called to give witness, and I wish to give it. The Lord God has granted that I have come to very closely know people who have given their whole lives to save life.

We hear the Savior of the world say: "Whatever you do to the least of my brethren, you do unto me." *(Mt. 25:40)*. He says this to each woman and mother, to each man and father, and to each doctor who has been called to protect life and health. He says this to all of us—those sitting in the world's parliaments, and those resting in the seclusion of their family homes. He says this to people everywhere.

Direct yourself to the God of Life. He is the only way of salvation available to us. Listen again to Pope John Paul II, who, throughout his pontificate, exhorted us to "open the doors to Christ!"

When we ponder the question of what prospects lie ahead for the coming century and for the next millennium, a thorough answer ought to be based on a profound hope.

The Polish people are now living in their own land—a land which has no price to it. We can breathe in its history and share it with Europe and the world at large. We continue to develop the culture we have accumulated down the centuries, and hand it on to the next generations. We herald the coming of the twenty-first century and later centuries to follow, marking each with Christ's Cross as we have ever since the day of Mieszko I (the first historical ruler of Poland), and singing the anthem, "Bogarodzica (Theotokos)," meaning "Mother of God."

Numerous undocumented sacrifices of the past century were made by several extraordinary figures. It was during this time that a Polish priest was elevated to the See of Peter, and it is this Pope who came to lead the Church, the world, and Poland into the new century and the new millennium. There is no need to hide our feelings here. Such is the untold pride of our country, Poland.

We have lasted through indescribable oppression, and we shall continue to live on; for we look to a future which has been underpinned by a great treasury of spiritual values, and of love for God and for the country He has given us.

Down the centuries our Savior has repeated to us, as he did on the Cross: "Behold your Mother," and He shall continue to point to His Mother Mary.

Let us prove ourselves worthy to be her children.

Archbishop Kazimierz Majdański
On the fifty-fourth anniversary of Dachau's liberation

The Dachau Camp Gate. "Work will set you free."

The Dachau Camp.

The "New crematory" in Dachau.

Pile of dead bodies before the crematory.

A prisoner who tried to escape.

Died of exhaustion.

The torments.

Miracle of liberation. The Holy Family in
St. Joseph's Sanctuary in Kalisz (Calissia).

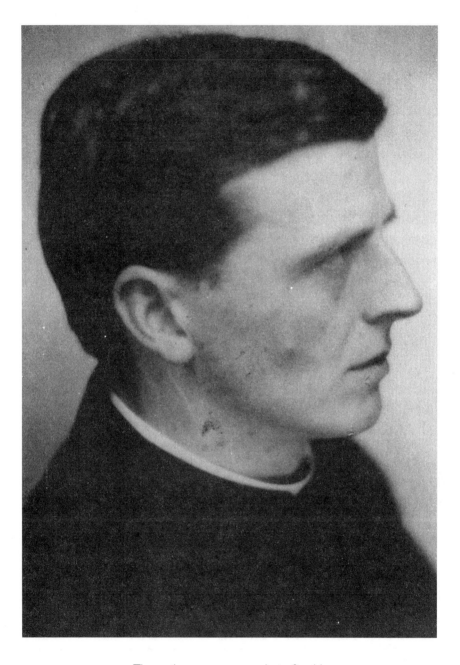

The author as a young priest after his
liberation from Dachau—Paris 1945.

The author during Holy Mass
in Dachau on June 20, 1989.

The homily during the Holy Mass
in Dachau on June 20, 1989.

In the Chapel of Thanksgiving and Martyrdom in Kalisz.

In Kalisz on April 29, 1970, on the
twenty-fifth anniversary of Dachau's liberation.

Celebrations marking the anniversary
of the liberation of Dachau.

The pilgrimage to Rome of ex-inmate priests and bishops on the fiftieth anniversary of the Priesthood of Pope Paul VI. The first station: Dachau. The Holy Mass in the Chapel of Christ's Mortal Fear in May of 1970. (The author is standing near the altar on the left).

Pilgrimage of ex-inmate priests and bishops. The audience with the Holy
Father Paul VI. In Rome the pilgrimage was headed by Cardinal Wojtyla.
(The author is the second from the left in the first line).

The author with Pope John Paul II.

The commemorative plaque on the outer wall of the Chapel
of Christ's Mortal Fear. The inscription in Polish, English, French, and German:
"Here in Dachau every third victim tormented to death was a Pole, and one in
every two Polish priests imprisoned here laid down his life. Their sacred memory
is venerated by their fellow prisoners, members of the Polish clergy."

The author with Cardinal Stefan Wyszyński, the Primate of Poland.

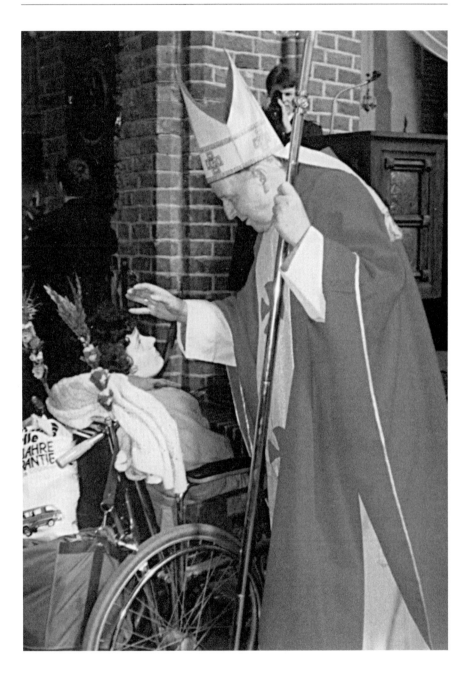

The author as a bishop of Szczecin-Kamień in the Szczecin cathedral.

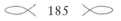

The author in a procession in Szczecin.

The author—always showing concern for the family.

The author with students of the Institute of Studies on the Family.

Meetings in the Family Center in Wiselka on the Baltic Coast.

Endnotes

1. Blessed Michael Kozal (1893–1943). He was the Auxiliary Bishop of Wloclawek from 1939. He martyred in Dachau concentration camp, and was
beatified in 1987.

2. St. Maximilian Maria Kolbe (1894–1941). A Franciscan priest, he was a
doctor of philosophy, founder of the Militia of the Immaculate and of monas-
teries in Niepokalanów, Poland and Nagasaki, Japan, and founder and editor-in-chief of the journals *Rycerz Niepokalanej* ("Knight of the Immaculate")
and *Maly Dziennik* ("Little Daily"). Father Kolbe volunteered to take the
place of a fellow inmate, a father of a family, in a starvation bunker in the
Auschwitz concentration camp. He was canonized on October 8, 1982.

3. It is important to realize that the Nazi regime intended not just to clear
Europe of Jews. Hitler's faithful Minister of Propaganda, Joseph Goebbels,
characterized the Nazi view of the Polish nation as follows: "The Fuehrer's
verdict on the Poles is damning. More like animals than human beings, completely primitive, stupid, and amorphous. And a ruling class that is an unsat-
isfactory result of a mingling between the lower orders and an Aryan master
race. The Poles' dirtiness is unimaginable. Their capacity for intelligent judg-
ment is absolutely nil. . . . The Fuehrer has no intention of assimilating the
Poles. . . . Had Henry the Lion conquered the East . . . the result could certainly have been a strongly slavicized race of German mongrels. Better the
present situation. Now we know the laws of racial heredity and can handle
things accordingly" (*Goebbels Diaries*, p.16).

4. Venerable Stefan Wyszynski (1909–1981). He was named Archbishop of
Gniezno and Warsaw in 1941, and he became Cardinal in 1953. He was a
stalwart defender of the Polish nation's Christian identity throughout the

Communist repression. Interred by the Communist authorities (1953–1956), his prison diaries are available in English translation. He was renowned for his preaching on patriotism, the dignity of women, and the sanctity of life, as well as for his love of Our Lady. The cause for his beatification is now underway in Rome, the diocesan stage having just recently been completed.

5. *Redemptor Hominis,* 8 & 16

6. cf. John Paul II, Auschwitz, June 7, 1979

7. The Gleiwitz incident was a staged attack on August 31, 1939 against the German radio station located in Gleiwitz, Germany (since 1945: Gliwice, Poland). This provocation was a Nazi SS project intended to create the appearance of Polish aggression against Germany, which was then used to justify the subsequent invasion of Poland.

8. *Ziemia Gromadzi Prochy* ("The Earth Is Collecting Ashes"), by Joseph Kisielewski. Ksiegarnia sw. Wojciecha, Poznan 1939. Reprint by PAX Warszawa 1990. An important historical work, it provides a detailed account of the author's impressions from his travels in the Third Reich just before the outbreak of the war. It says much about the far-reaching effects of the Nazi propaganda machine.

9. St. Stanislaw of Szczepanów (1030–1079). Bishop of Kraków, Stanislaw was martyred by King Boleslaw II ('Smialy') in the church at Skalka while saying Mass. The king was angered by the bishop's unrelenting pleas for morality, and his condemnation of adultery. The holy bishop insisted that the king must also be subject to the law of God, and criticized the King's unjust practices, his adulterous relationship with a married woman, and the bad influence he exerted on his subjects. The bishop also criticized the king for jeopardizing the family life of his soldiers by keeping them occupied with maneuvers in excess of several years at a time. The slaying of St. Stanislaw proved pivotal to Polish history. The nation forced the unjust king to flee, and the false Byzantine precept that morality does not apply to politics, a belief which held much ground in subsequent German history, was once and for all denounced by the Polish consciousness. St. Stanislaw was canonized in 1253, and subsequently played an important role in the unification of Poland. He is venerated as Patron of Poland, alongside St. Wojciech (Aldalbertus). In the United States alone there are more than sixty churches bearing this saint's name.

10. This could prove a rewarding task for historians to undertake, especially historians of the Wloclawek diocese.

11. The Jagiellonian University was founded in Kraków in 1364 by King Casimir the Great, and then reorganized to include a faculty of theology by St. Jadwiga, Queen of Poland. It is, to date, one of the most important centers of Polish culture and learning.

12. Fr. Józef Bochenski, O.P. (1902–1995). He was a Dominican priest of Polish extraction, a logician, and an analytical philosopher. He was also a Professor at Freiburg University in Switzerland (and Rector from 1964 to 1966), and was known for flying airplanes, as well.

13. The Collegium Novum was built from 1873–1887, and is the main building of the Jagiellonian University located in Kraków, Poland.

14. *Memories from the Sachsenhausen Camp, 1939/1940*, Warsaw, 1966, p. 74

15. The Battle of Vienna (September 12, 1683). This battle is a landmark of European history. Through it, Ottoman expansion into Europe was decisively checked. Despite being far outnumbered, the King of Poland, John III Sobieski, led a Christian coalition army to victory over the Ottoman army. The Ottoman Turks had been besieging Vienna for over two months, and moreover, they were openly planning to proceed on to Rome. Sobieski's feat not only liberated Vienna, but it also stalled this Islamic incursion down the Danube into the heartland of Europe. The Emperor of the Holy Roman Empire and his German princes, meanwhile, were tied up with their own domestic quarrels. Historians consider this to be one of the world's greatest battles, and the Church has since designated September 12 as the Feast of the Most Holy Name of Mary, in thanksgiving for the lifting of the Ottoman threat.

16. *The Auschwitz Cahiers,* Book 2, p. 33

17. *Ciernowa Mitra,* Warsaw 1971, p. 20 ff.

18. Wladyslaw Reymont is among Poland's best-known Polish authors. He won the Nobel Prize in 1924 for his novel *Chlopi,* meaning, "The Peasant," which is a masterful depiction of Polish rural village life following the cycle of the seasons.

19. Father Wiktor Jacewicz, S.D.B., *Martyrologium polskiego Duchowienstwa Rzymskokatolickiego Pod Okupacja Hitlerowska w Latach 1939–1945,* Warsaw 1977, Book I, p. 33)

20. The Schönstatt Movement is a Roman Catholic Marian Movement founded by Joseph Kentenich in Germany in 1914. It emphasizes a strong devotion to the Blessed Virgin Mary, upholding her as a perfect example of

love and purity. Today the movement is present in many countries besides Germany, and there are now more than one million people involved.

21. *Ateneum Kaplanskie /The Priestly Athenaeum,* Issue 374–375, p. 52.

22. St. Otto of Bamburg (1060 or 1061–1139). He was a German bishop and statesman, and also chaplain to Prince Vladislaus II Herman, and chancellor of Emperor Henry IV. He Christianized Pomerania (the Baltic Sea coastlands) under the reign of Boleslaus III Krzywousty.

23. A fuller account of this pilgrimage has already been published in a double issue of *Ataneum Kaplanskie* (nos. 374–375, p. 208), the article entitled: "Two Anniversaries."

24. *Dachau 1933–1945,* Katowice 1968, 2nd edition, p.199.

25. Saint Jadwiga of Slask (Saint Hedwig of Silesia) (1174–1243). She was the wife of Prince Henry I the Bearded, and mother of Prince Henry II the Pious. She founded several convents and became a Cistercian nun herself in 1220 in Trzebnica. Cardinal Wojtyla was elected Pope on her liturgical feast day, October 16, 1979.

26. Saint Cyril (827–869), and Saint Methodius (826–885). They were brothers, missionaries in Moravia, and men of learning. They devised the first Slavic alphabet (the Glagolitic alphabet), translated the Scriptures into Slavic, devised a Slavic liturgy, and are also known to have traveled between Byzantium, Rome, and Baghdad. Both Saint Cyril and Saint Methodius are Patron Saints of Europe, along with Saint Benedict.

27. *Martyrologium Romanum* ("Roman Martyrology") is the official Martyrology of the Roman Rite of the Roman Catholic Church. It provides an extensive, but not exhaustive, list of the saints recognized by the Church.

About the Author

Archbishop Kazimierz Majdański was born in Poland on March 1, 1916, as the youngest of thirteen children. While studying under Cardinal Stefan Wyszynski as a young seminarian, he and thousands of other Polish clergy were arrested by the Nazis in 1939 during the Second World War. Majdański was imprisoned in Sachsenhausen and Dachau, and was not liberated until April of 1945. In November of that same year, he was ordained Priest of Wloclawek, Poland.

In 1963, Majdański was consecrated as a bishop, and he became Bishop of the Diocese of Szczecin-Kamien from 1979 until he was appointed Archbishop in 1992. In recognition of his contribution towards Polish-German reconciliation, Majdański was awarded the highest German distinction that can be conferred on foreigners. Throughout his life, he showed great concern for the situation of the family in Poland and throughout the world. In 1975, he founded the Institute of Studies on the Family—the first such academic institute in the world.

A priest for sixty-one years and a bishop for forty-four, Archbishop Majdański died at the age of ninety-one on April 29, 2007—the same day as the sixty-second anniversary of Dachau's liberation, and the same year as the thirty-second anniversary of the founding of the Institute of Studies on the Family. He was the author of over thirty books and approximately 350 articles. *You Shall Be My Witnesses* has been published in Polish, Italian, Spanish, German, French, and now, in English.

Index